ACE The Pitch

Crafting the Deck that Opens Doors to Capital

DAYAKAR PUSKOOR

Published by F70Labs LLC

WHY I WROTE THIS BOOK

In the landscape of entrepreneurial guidance, much attention is given to the structural elements of pitch decks - the slides, the data, the metrics. However, while these are undeniably important, they only touch the surface of what can truly make a pitch resonate with investors. I noticed a profound gap in existing resources: the crucial but often overlooked aspects like the entrepreneur's mindset, the art of storytelling, understanding the venture ecosystem, and effectively communicating the investment opportunity beyond simple business potential.

"Ace the Pitch" was conceived as a manifesto for navigating these complex dimensions. It delves into the psychological readiness required to stand confidently before seasoned investors and make a memorable impression. I explore how strategic storytelling transforms a routine presentation into an engaging narrative that captivates and persuades, going beyond facts and figures to connect on an emotional level.

In addition to addressing these advanced elements, this guide does not overlook the foundational aspects of pitch preparation. I provide a thorough coverage of all traditional elements that should be included in a pitch. Each component is broken down with detailed explanations on how to maximize clarity and impact, ensuring that entrepreneurs can lay a solid groundwork before elevating their presentation with the unique approaches covered in the book.

Furthermore, this guide demystifies the venture world, offering a clear view of what investors look for, beyond the numbers. It teaches entrepreneurs how to handle objections with poise and discusses the critical follow-up actions after the pitch that keep the momentum going.

Most importantly, the book re-focuses the call to action by shifting the ultimate objective towards selling a piece of ownership in the company in exchange for financing, emphasizing how to position a business as a prime opportunity for attractive investor returns.

Perspectives

The Entrepreneur's Angle

Hello, visionaries and game-changers!

Throughout my journey of leading companies to success stories, I've seen firsthand the power of a pitch that does more than inform - it inspires. "Ace the Pitch" distills years of front-line experience into key strategies for crafting a narrative that resonates deeply with investors. It's about presenting your vision in a way that excites, persuades, and most importantly, converts interest into investment.

I guide you through weaving your entrepreneurial dreams into compelling stories that highlight not just the viability of your business but its potential to revolutionize the market.

The Investor's Perspective

Welcome to the other side of the table, where decisions are made, and futures are funded.

Having directed successful venture capital firms and propelled tech startups to their peak potential, I've recognized that what truly distinguishes a successful pitch is often the entrepreneur's ability to align with the investor's mindset. Through "Ace the Pitch," I share insights into the investor's perspective, revealing how to tailor your pitch to highlight not only the potential for success but also the strategic alignment with investor goals for long-term growth and profitability.

This book is your blueprint to understanding and leveraging the investor psychology that underpins funding decisions.

Dayakar Puskoor: https://www.linkedin.com/in/dayakarp/

FOREWORD

By Arun Ramamoorthy, Investor, Founding Partner, Z5 Capital

Having spent over a decade listening to pitches and collaborating with entrepreneurs, I've come to recognize the pitch as the art of storytelling that every entrepreneur needs to master. It's not just about securing funding; it's about forging partnerships, recruiting top talent, and getting customers excited about the business.

"Ace the Pitch" by Dayakar Puskoor is a comprehensive guide designed to transform how founders present their businesses to investors.

Drawing from his extensive career as a Microsoft executive and investor, Puskoor shares valuable insights gained from guiding companies. He emphasizes what truly resonates with investors: a compelling narrative, clarity of vision, and a well-crafted story. He breaks down the essential components of a winning pitch deck, from understanding the venture capital mindset to highlighting the significance of storytelling and emotional engagement.

Entrepreneurs are guided through each step of pitch preparation, receiving insights on how to align their business vision with market opportunities, structure financials for investor appeal, and anticipate and respond effectively to challenging questions from potential backers.

In the competitive world of startups, a compelling pitch can be the difference between success and failure. This book goes beyond a traditional handbook on pitch decks, delving into the strategic and psychological aspects of pitching that transcend data and slides.

"Ace the Pitch" is an essential read for entrepreneurs seeking to captivate investors, and investors seeking to comprehend the mechanics of pitches that convert presentations into successful partnerships.

By Kedar Kulkarni, Co-founder & CEO, HyperVerge

Dayakar has been an investor and board member of HyperVerge since 2014. He has seen HyperVerge transform from a rag-tag team of college kids to a conscious business.

What makes Dayakar stand out compared to a typical VC is his hands-on approach to helping investee companies, his tremendous energy, and his ability to build a team full of amazing people, all of whom bring complementary skill sets, yet work towards the common purpose of truly helping them get off the ground.

I wish this book was there when we made our first pitch! For most entrepreneurs, their first round of funding is a make-or-break moment. It is a time when the entrepreneur is still a rookie, learning the basics of building a business.

A pitch is such a crucial part of securing that first round of funding. When it goes really well, investors have even committed to investing just over a cup of coffee, and when it doesn't go well, we all know what happens on the long journey back home. There is no one right way to make a pitch work. And that is the difficult part.

Through "Ace the Pitch," Dayakar tries to explain the process, the do's and don'ts, and most importantly, as a VC, he really opens up about what an investor may be looking for. He has collected many invaluable nuggets of wisdom from hearing hundreds of pitches.

It is a great resource for a founder who just got started with an exciting idea and is now stepping into the world of investors where they are supposed to know everything! A great pitch prepares brave founders for the first of many trials that await them on this journey!

HOW TO USE THIS BOOK

Welcome to "Ace the Pitch", your comprehensive guide to mastering the art of the pitch deck and securing venture capital. This book is designed to be a step-by-step manual that transforms your entrepreneurial vision into a compelling narrative capable of attracting investors.

Here's how to effectively navigate and utilize the book for maximum benefit:

Step 1: Understand the Structure
Begin by familiarizing yourself with the structure of the book. Each chapter builds upon the previous, guiding you through different aspects of crafting a pitch and understanding the venture capital environment. Review the table of contents to get an overview of the topics covered, which will serve as a roadmap for your journey through the book.

Step 2: Read Thoroughly
Dive into each chapter to grasp the essentials of each topic. Focus particularly on the chapters that resonate with your current stage in the venture process. From psychological tactics in pitching to detailed breakdowns of financial structures, each chapter is packed with detailed explanations and expert tips.

Step 3: Apply the Lessons
After reading, begin applying what you've learned to your own pitch. Start with the foundational elements such as your business model and value proposition, detailed in early chapters. Use the checklists provided to help organize and refine your pitch materials.

Step 4: Draft Your Pitch Deck
Use the frameworks and insights from the book to start crafting your pitch deck, guided by Chapter 4, "The Anatomy of a Winning Pitch Deck." and Chapter 6 “The Pitch Deck”. These chapters help ensure that each slide of your deck effectively communicates your business vision, market opportunity, and strategy.

Step 5: Seek Feedback
Gather feedback from peers, mentors, and industry experts. Utilize their insights to polish your deck. The book's Chapter 5, "Crafting Your Story," offers valuable advice on how to effectively tell your business narrative, which can be crucial when seeking constructive criticism.

Step 6: Practice Your Pitch
Rehearse your pitch delivery to build confidence and refine your presentation skills. Chapter 7 offers techniques to engage your audience, ensuring you're prepared to deliver a compelling pitch.

Step 7: Use It as a Reference
Keep "Ace the Pitch" as a go-to reference as you refine your business strategy and continue pitching to investors. As your business evolves, revisit the chapters, case studies, templates, and checklists to align your pitch with new developments and market opportunities.

Conclusion
"Ace the Pitch" is designed to be a comprehensive partner in your quest for funding. By following these steps, you are not just preparing a pitch deck but laying the groundwork for your business's future success. Embrace this process, and let this book guide you from concept to successful pitch.

TABLE OF CONTENTS

CHAPTER 1: THE PSYCHOLOGICAL EDGE IN WINNING INVESTORS

"Embrace the power of mindset in pitching: where resilience meets persuasion, transforming every challenge into a stepping stone towards securing your vision's future."

Introduction

Imagine stepping into a brightly lit room, your eyes meeting those of a panel of potential investors. Your heart races as you recall the meticulously prepared pitch that you have rehearsed over the past days. This is more than just a presentation; it's a psychological game where your success depends not only on your business idea but also on your ability to manage and project your psychological state. This chapter explores how mastering the psychological approach can be as critical as the business plan when securing investment. It examines the scientific and emotional strategies that transform a routine pitch into a compelling story, one that captivates and convinces investors to believe in the vision..

Section 1: The Power of Mindset

Growth Mindset

Embracing a growth mindset is fundamental when facing investors. This mindset involves a belief in your capacity to learn and adapt, crucial in responding dynamically during a pitch. It's about showing potential investors that you are resilient and capable of overcoming future challenges.

Psychological and Physiological Synchronization

The congruency between your thoughts and body language sends a powerful message to your audience. A nervous presenter can undermine the confidence investors might have in the pitch. Conversely, synchronicity in what you say and how you present it, through controlled breathing, steady voice, and calm demeanor, can significantly enhance your message's persuasiveness.

Section 2: Psychological Strategies to Engage Investors

Building Trust and Engagement

Trust is the cornerstone of any relationship and is pivotal when convincing investors. Simple tactics like using terms that evoke familiarity and safety can help form an instant connection. For example, using inclusive language such as "we" and "our" can subconsciously align your goals with those of the investors, making your success their success.

The Role of Body Language

Non-verbal cues often speak louder than words. Maintaining eye contact, nodding to acknowledge points, and smiling naturally can help form a bond with your audience. These signals suggest honesty and confidence, both critical in a high-stakes investor pitch.

Section 3: The Science of Influence

Brain Chemistry in Sales

Understanding how the brain reacts during a pitch can give you an edge. Neurochemicals like dopamine and oxytocin can be stimulated by the way you deliver your pitch. For instance, presenting something unexpected or novel can trigger dopamine, which heightens attention and interest.

Creating a Balance of Desire and Tension

Craft your pitch to introduce elements of both desire and tension. Start with something that grabs attention, such as an intriguing statistic or a short story relevant to your business. Then, introduce a problem or tension point that your business aims to solve, keeping investors engaged and eager to hear the solution.

Section 4: Designing Your Pitch for Maximum Impact

Integrating Humor and Compassion

Humor, when used wisely, can ease tension and make you appear more approachable. It can be a strategic tool in making your pitch memorable.

CHAPTER 2: IMPORTANCE OF PITCH DECKS IN SECURING VENTURE CAPITAL

"A pitch deck is more than a tool; it's the narrative that weaves your vision, market potential, and unique value into a story that captures and holds investor interest from start to finish."

Introduction

Pitch decks are indispensable communication tools for entrepreneurs aiming to capture the attention and secure the investment of venture capitalists. These concise presentations serve as the primary vehicle for conveying the essence of a business to potential investors. When crafted skillfully, a pitch deck not only introduces your business but also becomes a pivotal element in the fundraising process, making the difference between securing the funding necessary for growth or missing a critical opportunity to advance your startup.

Section 1: The Role of Pitch Decks

First Impressions Count

In the competitive world of startups, the initial impression your pitch deck makes can significantly influence an investor's perception and interest. A well-prepared pitch deck must be polished, professional, and compelling, offering a clear and engaging snapshot of your company. This first interaction is crucial as it sets the tone for all subsequent discussions and can fundamentally shape the trajectory of your investment conversations.

Narrative and Storytelling

More than just a set of slides, a pitch deck weaves a compelling narrative about your company. It should clearly articulate what your business does, the problems it aims to solve, and how it distinguishes itself in the marketplace. Effective storytelling in a pitch deck encapsulates the mission, vision, and unique value proposition of your startup, helping to engage and resonate emotionally with potential investors.

Data Presentation

Pitch decks must efficiently communicate key data points such as market size, business model viability, competitive analysis, and financial projections. This information should be presented clearly and persuasively, with a focus on how the data supports the business case. Utilizing visuals like charts, graphs, and infographics, a well-designed pitch deck translates complex data into accessible insights, illustrating the potential return on investment and underscoring the scalability of the business.

Engagement and Discussion Starter

The ultimate goal of a pitch deck is to spark interest and initiate dialogue. It should be designed to not only inform but also engage viewers by prompting questions and discussions about various aspects of the business. This engagement is crucial for building rapport and trust with potential investors, providing an avenue to delve deeper into your business model, the expertise of your team, and your growth strategy.

Section 2: Importance in Securing Venture Capital

Screening Tool

Venture capitalists encounter a high volume of investment opportunities, making pitch decks an essential screening tool. A compelling pitch deck conveys your startup's potential and fit with an investor's portfolio, allowing it to stand out in a crowded marketplace. The clarity and effectiveness of a pitch deck often determine whether a startup progresses to more detailed stages of due diligence.

Competitive Edge

In the highly competitive startup ecosystems, your pitch deck is your chance to differentiate your business from the competition. It should highlight the unique strengths and advantages of your startup, providing clear and compelling reasons for investors to consider your venture as a preferable investment opportunity.

Fundraising Catalyst

An effective pitch deck does more than just communicate information; it acts as a catalyst in the fundraising process. It's often the basis for securing initial meetings with investors and plays a crucial role throughout the investment rounds. A persuasive pitch deck demonstrates your business's scalability, the capability of your team, and the expansiveness of the market opportunity, directly influencing investment decisions and potentially leading to successful funding.

Conclusion

Ultimately, the pitch deck serves as your startup's ambassador. It is the opening dialogue in what you hope will become a fruitful investment relationship.

By concisely packaging your business strategy, market analysis, and growth potential, a well-crafted pitch deck not only persuades but also convinces potential investors of the merits of your venture.

As such, understanding the importance of a pitch deck and mastering the art of its creation are essential skills for any entrepreneur embarking on the venture capital journey.

"Ace the Pitch" is designed to guide you through this process, ensuring that you present your vision in the most compelling way possible, ready to engage the interest and secure the support of the venture capital community.

CHAPTER 3: UNDERSTANDING VENTURE CAPITAL

"Venture capital is not just about funding; it's about building strategic partnerships that fuel innovation, scalability, and long-term success in the dynamic startup ecosystem."

Introduction

Venture capital (VC) is a form of private equity and a type of financing that investors provide to startup companies that are believed to have long-term growth potential. For startups without access to capital markets, venture capital is an essential source of money.

However, venture capital is about more than just funding. VCs are looking for a return on investment, yes, but they also bring guidance, expertise, and an invaluable network to a startup.

VCs play a pivotal role in the startup ecosystem, often determining which innovations disrupt industries and which ones never make it off the ground. To successfully pitch to these influential players, you must not only present a compelling business idea but also align it with the VC's financial strategies and risk management frameworks.

This chapter delves into the core of how VCs operate, the mathematical rigor behind their decisions, and the strategic mindsets that drive their investments.

Section 1: Understanding VC Fund Structure and Economics

The Role of Investors and General Partners

Investors (Limited Partners or LPs): Typically consisting of large family offices, pension funds and other institutions, these entities allocate a small percentage (often 2-5%) of their capital to venture capital due to its high-risk, high-return nature. Limited Partners typically have limited involvement but share in the financial returns.

General Partners (GPs): These individuals manage the VC firm and its funds, securing commitments from LPs with the promise of returns, and they earn through management fees and carried interest (carry) contingent on successful exits. General Partners are responsible for identifying potential investments, conducting due diligence, and providing strategic support to portfolio companies.

The 2 - 20 Rule: Economics of a VC Firm
VC firms generally charge a 2% management fee annually and aim for a 20% carry on the returns generated beyond the expectations of the LPs. For example, in this case, on a $100 million fund over 10 years, $20 million would cover operational costs, leaving $80 million investible.

Section 2: The Investment Math: Scenarios and Outcomes

Investment Distribution and Exit Scenarios

VCs typically diversify their investments across multiple stages (Pre-Seed, Seed, Series A, Series B, Series C+), adjusting the amount invested considering the fund dynamics.

Scenario Analysis: Various exit scenarios illustrate the challenges in achieving desired returns. For instance, needing a 'unicorn' to realize sufficient returns underlines the high stakes and high risks involved in venture capital investments.

Understanding the financial mechanics and strategic considerations of VCs is essential for crafting pitches that resonate with their goals and risk profiles. Entrepreneurs who grasp these aspects can better position their startups as viable investments.

This chapter sets the stage for deeper insights into each strategic focus area, which will be explored in subsequent chapters, providing you with a comprehensive toolkit for navigating the venture capital landscape effectively.

Section 3: Types of VC Firms

Early-Stage VCs

These firms invest in companies in the early phases of their operations, where the risk is higher but so is the potential return. They typically invest in seed to Series A rounds, providing capital to help companies grow from concept to initial execution.

Growth-Stage VCs

These investors come in at a slightly later stage when the company has demonstrated some market success and is ready to scale. These firms often deal in larger amounts of capital and expect a faster turnaround on their investment.

Late-Stage VCs

Investment at this stage is typically safer and less about high growth rates and more about preparing the company for a public offering or acquisition. Companies are expected to have a clear path to profitability and a significant market share.

Section 4: The Mindset of Venture Capitalists

Venture capitalists are driven by the potential for high returns, which is often reflected in their investment strategy and decision-making process.

Here are some key insights into their mindset:

Return on Investment: At the core, VCs are looking for companies that can return their initial investment many times over. The typical venture capital investment occurs after the seed funding round as part of the early-stage funding of a company that has shown potential for rapid growth and profitability.

Risk and Reward: Venture capitalists often balance the high risk of early-stage investments against potential high rewards. They typically diversify their risk by investing in multiple startups across different industries.

Vision and Scalability: VCs are interested in businesses with a clear and compelling vision that have the potential to scale significantly. They look for innovative solutions that solve substantial problems in large markets.

Management Team: The quality, experience, and dedication of a startup's management team is critically important. VCs often invest in the team as much as the product or business model itself.

De-risking at Various Funding Stages: Investments typically extend from pre-seed through various funding rounds like Series A, B, C, etc. Here's how venture capitalists focus on mitigating potential pitfalls at each stage:

Pre-Seed Stage
Challenge: Technical Viability
Goal: Establish that the product or service is technically viable.
Areas of Attention:

- Create a basic, workable model of the product (MVP).
- Validate the functionality of the underlying technology.
- Start assembling the foundational team.

Seed Stage
Challenge: Market Fit
Goal: Confirm that the product meets a real market need.
Areas of Attention:

- Enhance the MVP using feedback from initial users.
- Define the primary market and identify specific customer segments.
- Set up initial metrics for tracking user growth and engagement.

Series A Stage
Challenge: Market Entry and Penetration
Goal: Formulate and execute a strategy for market entry and growth.
Areas of Attention:

- Strengthen the team by adding sales and marketing professionals.
- Broaden the customer base to validate and refine the business model.
- Evaluate financial metrics like customer acquisition costs and unit economics.

Series B Stage
Challenge: Market Expansion
Goal: Prove the product's scalability in broader markets.
Areas of Attention:

- Enhance operational capabilities and infrastructure to spur growth.
- Broaden the range of products or venture into new markets.
- Fine-tune and expand the sales and marketing strategies.

Series C+ Stage
Challenge: Organizational Culture
Goal: Preserve and develop the company culture amid expansion.
Areas of Attention:

- Focus on nurturing the company culture and developing staff.
- Ensure the leadership is equipped to handle a growing workforce.
- Keep the company's core values and vision intact as the organization scales.

Section 5: The Venture Capital Investment Process

Identifying Opportunities
Venture capitalists uncover investment opportunities through various channels such as referrals, incoming proposals, and proactive searches at industry gatherings and pitching events.

Evaluative Scrutiny
In this critical phase, venture capitalists undertake an exhaustive examination of the startup's business strategy, market potential, product effectiveness, competitive landscape, and the proficiency of the management team.

Decision Framework
The investment decision is shaped by the findings from the due diligence phase and considers factors like expected returns, associated risks, and the alignment with the venture capitalist's strategic investment objectives.

Here's a breakdown of the decision-making hierarchy and process:

Understanding Roles within the Firm: It is essential to recognize the different partners within the firm, particularly distinguishing between 'investment partners' who are pivotal in decision-making and other partners whose roles might not directly influence investment choices. The influence of each partner on a deal's progression varies significantly.

Decision-Making Dynamics: Firms differ in their approach to making investment decisions. Some operate on a consensus basis, requiring broad agreement, whereas others rely on the strong opinion of a single partner who champions the deal. Additionally, the presence of supporting partners who support the primary partner can sway decisions.

Influence of Non-Partner Staff: Though they do not make final decisions, non-partner staff such as Analysts, Associates, and Principals are integral in sourcing opportunities, conducting preliminary evaluations, performing due diligence, and contributing insights during discussions. Their level of influence can vary across firms.

Strategy Meetings: These are usually scheduled for Mondays and are critical for decision-making. Founders present their pitches, and the partner who sponsors the deal presents their investment thesis. The atmosphere can be highly charged, with feedback ranging from enthusiastic endorsements to critical evaluations. The process might include voting, discussions led by a dominant partner, or even a veto mechanism.

Broadening Engagement: Founders should endeavor to cultivate relationships with multiple influential people within the firm, not just the primary partner or associate managing their deal. Impressions made on other partners and key staff before the decisive meeting can markedly enhance the prospects of securing investment. A nuanced understanding of these internal dynamics can significantly refine a founder's approach to securing venture capital, tailoring their pitch to resonate with the unique decision-making culture of the firm.

Conclusion

Understanding the mindset of venture capitalists and the stages of venture capital can greatly enhance an entrepreneur's strategy for securing investment. By recognizing what is typically de-risked at various funding stages and adjusting their business strategies accordingly, startups can better position themselves as attractive investment opportunities. Knowing the types of VC firms and what they look for can help tailor pitches and development plans to meet these criteria, thereby increasing the chances of successful funding.

This chapter provides an overview of the venture capital ecosystem, a critical engine of growth for innovative startups and small businesses around the world. Understanding the nuances of how venture capital functions, from the types of VC firms to the intricate process of making investment decisions, equips you with the knowledge to better navigate your entrepreneurial journey and effectively engage with potential investors.

A good grasp of the various stages of VC funding, from pre-seed to late-stage, reveals the different risk assessments and strategic inputs required at each phase. This helps startups align their business development stages with the expectations of potential investors, ensuring they are better prepared to meet these criteria and secure funding. Additionally, the insights into the mindset of venture capitalists, including the balance of risk and reward, the importance of scalability, and the value of a solid management team, are invaluable. These highlight the importance of not just having a robust business idea but also demonstrating the potential for significant growth and market disruption.

Entrepreneurs armed with this knowledge can craft pitch decks that not only highlight the value of their innovations but also resonate deeply with the investment philosophy and criteria of potential venture capital partners, significantly boosting their chances of securing the necessary capital to propel their visions to reality.

CHAPTER 4: THE ANATOMY OF A WINNING PITCH DECK

"Crafting a winning pitch deck is an art of precision and storytelling, where each slide builds a cohesive narrative that showcases your vision, market opportunity, and strategic roadmap to captivate investors."

Section 1: Essential Components of a Pitch Deck

Creating an effective pitch deck is not just about providing information; it's about crafting a story that resonates with your audience, particularly investors who are constantly on the lookout for compelling business opportunities. While Chapter 6 will delve into the specifics of each slide in a pitch deck, it's crucial to first grasp the overarching structure and elements that form the backbone of an effective presentation. This chapter provides a detailed overview of the essential components of a pitch deck, designed to convey your business vision, market opportunity, and strategy in a concise, compelling, and visually engaging manner.

Here, we elaborate on the core elements that every entrepreneur needs to master to build a foundation for a successful pitch. A winning pitch deck efficiently communicates your business's vision, market opportunity, and strategy in a streamlined and visually engaging way.

Problem Framework:
This sets the stage by summarizing the critical aspects of your business. Include what your company does, the significant problems it addresses, and why this is the opportune moment for your solution. This section should grab attention and make it clear why your business stands out.

Business and Market Framework:
This demonstrates the viability of your business within the context of the broader market. Share key performance indicators, early traction data, and validations from customers, partners, or industry experts. This evidence supports your claim of market demand and potential for expansion.

Financials and Future Outlook:
This communicates the financial health and future prospects of your business. Present a clear view of your financial history (if applicable), projected revenues, and detailed funding needs. Explain how the investments will be used and the expected impact on the growth of your business.

Team and Leadership:
This establishes credibility by showcasing the strength and expertise of your team. Highlight the qualifications, experience, and roles of your key team members. Emphasize how their backgrounds and skills make them the right people to lead and grow the business.

Section 2: Common Mistakes and How to Avoid Them

Overwhelming the Audience: Ensure your pitch deck is concise. Focus on essential information to maintain clarity and impact without cluttering slides.

Lack of Coherent Narrative: Your pitch should flow logically, telling a compelling story that leads seamlessly to your call to action. Make sure each slide contributes to this narrative.

Underestimating Design Importance: The visual presentation can profoundly impact the reception of your pitch. Invest in professional design and maintain a consistent aesthetic throughout to enhance readability and engagement.

Skipping the 'Why': Always connect your business activities back to the core problem you are solving. Highlight the necessity and timeliness of your solution.

Neglecting the Ask: Be explicit about your funding needs. Clearly articulate how much money you need, how it will be used, and the expected returns for the investors.

CHAPTER 5: CRAFTING YOUR STORY

"The power of storytelling in business lies in its ability to transform data into a compelling narrative, turning your pitch from a presentation into an unforgettable experience that resonates with investors on an emotional and intellectual level."

Section 1: The Power of Storytelling in Business Pitches

Storytelling as a Strategic Tool

Storytelling in business is not merely about narrating events; it's a strategic tool that can profoundly influence decision-making. Through storytelling, entrepreneurs transform their pitches from static presentations into dynamic narratives that resonate deeply with their audience. This chapter explores the psychological underpinnings of why stories affect us so profoundly and provides a detailed framework for crafting an engaging narrative for your pitch.

Psychological Basis of Storytelling

Humans are wired to respond to stories. Neurological research suggests that when we hear a story, not only the language processing areas of our brains light up, but also those involved in experiencing the events. This phenomenon is known as neural coupling. Moreover, a well-told story can release oxytocin, the hormone associated with empathy and connection, which makes us more trusting and open to the storyteller's ideas. This is why stories can be such powerful tools in pitches - they foster a deeper, emotional connection with investors, which is crucial for persuasion.

Section 2: Elements of a Powerful Story

Setting the Stage: This establishes context and relevance. Start by explaining the origins of your startup. What sparked the idea? Was it a personal experience, an undeniable market gap, or a technological innovation? Anchor your narrative in a relatable context that highlights the necessity and timeliness of your solution.

Introducing Characters: This humanizes your story. Present your team and customers as the protagonists. For your team, focus on individual backgrounds, highlighting diverse expertise and a shared commitment to the vision. For customers, depict them as beneficiaries whose challenges are central to why your business exists. Their transformation through your product or service will serve as a testament to your impact.

Building the Plot: This serves to outline the journey and build tension. Narrate the evolution of your startup, from conception through to its current state. Include key milestones, such as pivotal decisions, major challenges, and how your team adapted and overcame these obstacles. This not only builds engagement but also showcases your resilience and adaptability.

Climax and Resolution: This delivers the payoff. Here, reveal the climax of your startup's story - the launch or planned launch of your solution. Detail how it addresses the problems outlined earlier and the beneficial changes it has brought or aims to bring to your target market.

Future Vision: This helps project forward and inspire. Conclude with a compelling vision of the future. Describe where you see your company heading, the potential market impact, and how you plan to scale. This not only underscores ambition but also solidifies the ongoing relevance and longevity of your venture.

Section 3: Crafting Your Narrative

Clarity and Simplicity:
Simplicity is key in communication. Use clear, jargon-free language that can easily be understood by someone outside your industry. This helps to ensure that your message is not lost in translation.

Emotional Engagement:
To connect on an emotional level, your story should tap into universal feelings: the struggle against adversity, the triumph of innovation, or the satisfaction of customer needs. Frame your narrative in a way that

highlights these emotional undertones, making your story resonate more deeply.

Utilizing Visuals:
Visual elements like charts, images, and videos can significantly enhance your story, making abstract concepts memorable. Use visuals that complement and amplify your narrative, rather than distract from it.

Consistency Across Channels:
Ensure that the core elements of your story remain consistent, whether you're pitching in person, in a video, or through written content. This consistency helps to build a strong, recognizable brand narrative.

Rehearsal and Refinement:
Practice your pitch multiple times to refine your storytelling and delivery. Each rehearsal should make your narrative smoother and your delivery more confident, ensuring that your passion for your venture shines through.

Section 4: Common Storytelling Mistakes to Avoid

Overcomplexity:
Keep your narrative focused and relevant. Avoid the temptation to include too much technical detail or too many tangential threads, which can confuse and disengage your audience.

Lacking Authenticity:
Authenticity is the cornerstone of effective storytelling. Ensure your narrative is genuine and reflective of your true mission and values.

Ignoring the Audience:
Adapt your story to your audience. Different investors may be motivated by different aspects of your business, such as technological innovation, market potential, or social impact. Tailor your story to align with their interests and investment philosophy.

Omitting the USP:

Your unique selling proposition should be clear and prominent within your narrative. It's what sets your startup apart from the competition and is critical to making your business memorable.

Conclusion

Effective storytelling in business pitches can significantly enhance how investors perceive and react to your presentation. By crafting a narrative that not only informs but also emotionally engages, you create a memorable pitch that stands out.

This chapter equips you with the tools to harness the power of storytelling, transforming your pitch from a simple presentation to a compelling narrative that captures the imagination and investment of your audience.

CHAPTER 6: THE PITCH DECK

"Your pitch deck is the blueprint of your business vision, meticulously designed to communicate your strategy, competitive edge, and growth potential, ultimately guiding investors towards a shared path of success."

Introduction

The pitch deck is more than just a presentation; it's the crystallization of your startup's vision, strategy, and potential. It serves as your first impression, your argument, and your proposal, all rolled into one. As such, creating a compelling pitch deck is one of the most crucial steps in your journey to secure venture capital. This chapter will guide you through each slide, explaining not only what to include but also how to effectively communicate your message to make a lasting impact on your audience. Your pitch deck should seamlessly combine data, design, and narrative to tell a persuasive story that captivates and convinces. It's not just about the information you present, but how you present it, making every slide count in building towards a compelling call to action. Whether you are addressing seasoned investors or newcomers to the venture scene, your deck must resonate on a fundamental level, appealing both to their analytical minds and their entrepreneurial spirits.

To begin, this chapter explores the anatomy of a pitch deck, detailing the purpose and key elements of each slide, from establishing the problem you solve, to outlining your business model, and ultimately, articulating your financial needs and future projections. Each section of this chapter is dedicated to one slide of your pitch deck, offering insights into crafting content that is both informative and inspiring. This discussion includes how to:

- Clearly define the market problem your startup is addressing, establishing the necessity for your solution (The Problem - Unveiling Market Gaps)

- Substantiate the market demand for your solution with research, data, and early user feedback (Market Validation - Confirming the Demand)
- Articulate how your product or service uniquely solves the identified problem and the benefits it offers (The Solution - Bridging the Gap)
- Outline your company's core philosophy, long-term vision, and operational mission (The Company - Vision and Mission)
- Describe the proprietary technology and intellectual property that differentiate your product (Technology & IP - Securing the Edge)
- Detail how your company will generate revenue, explaining the scalability and sustainability of your business model (Business Model - Sustaining Value Creation)
- Present your go-to-market strategy, illustrating how you plan to penetrate and grow in the market (GTM Motion - Entering the Market)
- Provide a competitive analysis, highlighting your strategic advantages and positioning in the market (The Competition - Outlining the Battlefield)
- Show early achievements and traction to illustrate market acceptance and potential growth (Market Traction - Demonstrating Early Success)
- Present financial projections and funding needs, detailing how investments will be utilized and the expected outcomes (The Financials - Mapping the Numbers)
- Identify and explain potential risks and your strategies for managing them (The Risks - Addressing Potential Hurdles)
- Discuss contingency plans for dealing with unexpected market or operational challenges (The Contingencies - Planning for Uncertainties)

- Introduce key team members, highlighting their expertise and roles in driving the company's growth (The Team - The Drivers of Success)

- Outline key milestones and goals that chart your company's path forward in the market (Target Milestones - Setting the Roadmap)

- Clearly specify the funding you are seeking, what it will be used for, and the potential returns for investors (The Ask - Securing Strategic Investment)

This structured approach to each slide, ensures that you provide a comprehensive view of your business, from the problem it solves to the strategic execution of your vision, culminating in a compelling call to action for investment. By the end of this chapter, you will have a structured blueprint for constructing a pitch deck that not only details every critical aspect of your business but does so in a way that is strategically aligned with investor expectations.

Prepare to transform your vision into a visually compelling and strategically persuasive pitch deck that stands out in the competitive venture capital landscape.

Slide 1: The Problem - Unveiling Market Gaps

Purpose:
This slide is foundational, aiming to clearly justify the existence of your startup by spotlighting a critical, unresolved market problem. It sets the stage for the entire presentation by contextualizing the need for your solution.

Content:
Introduction to the Problem: Begin with a gripping opening statement that effectively conveys the urgency and relevance of the problem. Expand by describing the problem in a manner that resonates not just locally but

globally, showcasing its impact across different market segments. Illustrate how this problem is a barrier to progress, efficiency, or cost-savings, thereby affecting customers' daily operations or quality of life.

Detailed Impact Analysis: Elaborate on how the problem impacts various stakeholders: consumers, businesses, and the industry at large. Use real-world examples, case studies, and narratives that paint a vivid picture of the challenges faced. Complement this with quantitative data such as financial losses, productivity dips, or market inefficiencies that reinforce the scale of the problem. This section should make the problem relatable and significant, ensuring it resonates with the audience's experiences or understanding.

Existing Solutions and Their Shortcomings: Provide a critical analysis of the current solutions available in the market. Detail these solutions and discuss their limitations, such as high costs, poor user experience, inefficacy, or inaccessibility. Explain how these solutions fail to meet the needs of the target market fully, thereby leaving a substantial gap that your startup is poised to fill. This comparison should highlight the inadequacies in current approaches and frame your solution as a superior alternative.

Visual Elements:

Impact Visuals: Employ powerful visuals that graphically illustrate the magnitude and scope of the problem. Consider using time-series graphs demonstrating the problem's growth over time, heat maps showing geographical dispersion, or comparative infographics that highlight the inadequacy of existing solutions. These visuals should be striking and memorable, designed to evoke a response and make the problem undeniably evident.

Quote or Testimonial: Incorporate a compelling quote from a recognized industry expert or a testimonial from a potential customer who has experienced the problem first-hand. This personal touch adds credibility and an emotional appeal, making the problem more tangible and urgent. Choose a quote that captures the essence of the problem and the need for an innovative solution.

Conclusion and Transition: While this slide focuses on defining the problem, conclude with a brief teaser of how your startup proposes to address this gap, setting the stage for the next slides. This transition should be smooth and natural, piquing interest in your solution without revealing too much too soon.

Slide 2: Market Validation - Confirming the Demand

Purpose: This slide aims to substantiate the market need for your solution through rigorous data analysis and research. By demonstrating robust market demand, it reinforces the viability and potential success of your startup in addressing a significant problem.

Content:

Market Research Highlights: Start with a robust presentation of market research findings that underscore the existence and magnitude of the problem your startup intends to solve. Include specific insights from surveys, focus groups, and market analysis reports. Highlight key statistics that reflect the urgency of addressing the issue, such as customer dissatisfaction levels, unmet needs, and the economic impact.

Detailed TAM, SAM, and SOM Analysis: Provide a thorough breakdown of the Total Addressable Market (TAM), Serviceable Available Market (SAM), and Serviceable Obtainable Market (SOM). Explain the methodology used to calculate these figures (Refer to Appendix A for a deep-dive on these):

TAM: The overall global or national revenue opportunity your product or service is aiming to capture.
SAM: The segment of TAM within your operational reach considering geographic and regulatory constraints.
SOM: The portion of SAM that you realistically aim to capture, given current market conditions and competitive landscape.

This section should not only present numbers but also discuss how these figures relate to real business opportunities and strategic planning.

Demand Evidence: Corroborate the market need with concrete evidence of demand:

Pre-orders and Pilot Tests: Share data on pre-orders or results from pilot tests that demonstrate early adopter enthusiasm and willingness to purchase.

Beta Testing Feedback: Provide insights from beta testing that highlight user satisfaction and product efficacy, emphasizing any high conversion rates or repeat usage statistics.

Letters of Intent: Mention any letters of intent or commitments from potential customers, which can serve as a strong indicator of market demand and future revenue.

Visual Elements:

Data Charts: Utilize well-designed charts to present the TAM, SAM, and SOM data. Use clear, contrasting colors to differentiate between these segments, ensuring that the information is accessible and easily digestible. These visuals should clearly outline the market potential and scope, making a strong case for the scalability of your solution.

Market Demand Graphics: Employ bullet points, icons, or small infographics to highlight critical data points about market demand. These visuals should focus on key statistics like market growth rates, customer acquisition costs, and potential market penetration rates. The design should be sleek and professional, reinforcing the data-driven approach of your startup.

Conclusion and Transition: Conclude this slide by summarizing how the data presented validates the demand for your solution, setting a confident tone for introducing your product or service in the following slides. This transition should be smooth, leading naturally into how your offering uniquely addresses the validated market needs.

Slide 3: The Solution - Bridging the Gap

Purpose:
This slide is crucial as it introduces your solution, explaining how it uniquely addresses and resolves the significant problem identified previously. The goal is to clearly articulate why your solution is not just viable but also superior to existing alternatives.

Content:
Solution Overview: Begin by describing your solution in detail, focusing on its unique approach to solving the identified problem. Explain the technology, methodology, or innovation at the core of your product or service. Highlight how this approach is different from anything currently available in the market. Provide context on how the solution was developed, including any research, technological advancements, or market insights that influenced its design.

Key Features and Benefits: Enumerate the key features of your solution, and directly connect each feature to a tangible benefit for the user or customer. For example, if a feature of your tech product is enhanced security, explain how this leads to greater user trust and safety. This section should clearly demonstrate how each feature addresses specific aspects of the problem outlined in Slide 1, thereby resolving those issues effectively.

Proof of Concept: If available, provide compelling evidence that demonstrates the effectiveness of your solution in real-world scenarios.

This could include:
Case Studies: Share success stories of early adopters who have benefited significantly from your solution.
Test Results: Present data from testing phases that show measurable improvements over existing solutions.
Customer Testimonials: Include quotes from beta testers or early customers that testify to the value and impact of your solution.

Visual Elements:

Solution Diagrams or Flowcharts: Use clear and informative diagrams or flowcharts to illustrate how your solution functions. These should detail the operational process or the technology behind your product, showing the step-by-step transformation from problem to resolution.

Before and After Scenarios: Employ visual comparisons to dramatically showcase the effectiveness of your solution. These could be graphical depictions of productivity levels, cost savings, time savings, or quality improvements, comparing the state before and after the adoption of your solution. This visual should be striking, aiming to make an instant visual impact that underscores the transformative power of your solution.

Interactive Elements (optional): Consider incorporating interactive elements like clickable demos or simulations that allow the viewer to experience the solution dynamically. This can be particularly effective in engaging potential investors and helping them understand the practical application and impact of your product or service.

Conclusion and Transition:

Wrap up by reaffirming how your solution is poised to revolutionize the market or drastically improve the status quo. Transition smoothly into the next section of your pitch.

Slide 4: The Company - Vision and Mission

Purpose:

This slide establishes the foundational principles of your startup, communicating what your company aims to achieve in the long run and the approach to getting there. It defines the core essence and strategic direction that guides all company activities and decision-making.

Content:

Vision Statement: Develop a visionary statement that encapsulates the 'Why' of your company, its reason for existence and the long-term impact it seeks to have on the world. The vision should be inspirational and aspirational, reflecting the ultimate impact you envisage. For example, if your startup is focused on educational technology, your vision could be: "To revolutionize the learning experience globally, making quality education accessible to everyone." This statement should not only be expansive and motivating but also paint a picture of the future your company is striving to create.

Mission Statement: Articulate your mission with a focus on the 'What' and 'How' - what your company does daily and how it plans to achieve its vision. This statement should be action-oriented, detailing the practical strategies and operational objectives. For example: "By developing user-friendly, scalable learning platforms, we enable educators to reach diverse learner populations effectively." Here, the use of "by" constructs provides clarity on how the company intends to realize its vision through specific actions.

Combining Vision and Mission into a Purpose Statement:
Sometimes, it might be beneficial to combine the vision and mission into a single, concise Purpose Statement. This approach can streamline your communication, making it easier for investors and stakeholders to grasp the essence of your company. For instance: "Our purpose is to revolutionize global education by providing scalable, accessible learning tools that empower educators and learners alike." This single statement expresses why the company exists, what it does, and how it plans to achieve its goals.

Visual Elements:
Vision and Mission Graphics: Use creative typography or compelling graphics to highlight your Vision, Mission, or unified Purpose Statement. These visual elements should be powerful and evoke the spirit of your company's goals, making them memorable and striking.

Alignment Illustrations: Incorporate diagrams or icons that visually demonstrate the alignment between your company's strategic objectives and market needs. These could include graphical representations like flowcharts that connect market needs directly to your business activities, showing how your operational strategies are geared towards achieving your vision.

Company Values (optional): Optionally, include a section on your company's core values, using icons or brief statements to illustrate how these values support both your vision and mission. This can highlight the cultural foundations that drive your business operations and strategic decisions.

Conclusion and Transition:
Conclude this slide by emphasizing that your company is built on a clear, compelling foundation that not only addresses current market needs but is also poised to shape the future of the industry. Transition smoothly into the next part of your pitch.

Slide 5: Technology & IP - Securing the Edge

Purpose:
This slide demonstrates the technological foundation and intellectual property that provide your startup with a competitive edge. It's vital to articulate how your innovations and IP rights protect your market position and enhance your product's unique value.

Content:
Technological Innovations: Detail your Key Technologies: Describe the critical technological components of your solution, highlighting any novel or proprietary aspects. Explain how these technologies solve the problem more effectively than existing solutions and provide specific metrics or results where possible.

Highlight Differentiation: Focus on what sets your technology apart from competitors. Emphasize unique features, performance enhancements, cost savings, or user benefits that your technology brings to the market.

Intellectual Property:
Patents: Describe any patents you have applied for or secured.

If applicable, distinguish between provisional and utility patents. Explain how these patents protect crucial aspects of your technology and the competitive advantage they provide.

Trademarks: List important trademarks associated with your brand, including logos, product names, or slogans. Explain how these trademarks are crucial for brand identity and how they are protected legally.

Copyrights: Mention any copyrights you hold, especially for software, written content, or unique designs. Clarify that copyright protection arises automatically upon creation and fixation in a tangible form, securing your original works from unauthorized use.

Geographical Scope: Discuss the territorial coverage of your IP rights. If your business operates or plans to operate internationally, mention steps taken to secure IP rights in key markets outside your home country.

Visual Elements:

Technology Diagrams: Include diagrams or flowcharts that explain how your technology works. These should be clear and detailed enough to illustrate the innovation behind your solution.

IP Certificates and Icons: Use icons to represent different types of IP (patents, trademarks, copyrights) and include visuals of any IP certificates. This helps to visually affirm the protected status of your technology and brand.

Roadmap Graphic: Show a timeline of your technology development and future IP milestones. This roadmap should highlight past technological advancements and outline upcoming initiatives to improve and expand your technological assets.

Conclusion and Transition:

Conclude by emphasizing the strategic importance of your technology and IP in securing a competitive position in the market. Transition smoothly into the next section of your pitch.

Slide 6: Business Model - Sustaining Value Creation

Purpose:
This slide is critical for illustrating how your startup will generate sustainable revenue. It should detail the business model itself, various revenue streams and demonstrate the scalability and sustainability of your business model, ensuring potential investors understand how your company will achieve financial success.

Content:
Business Model: In today's dynamic market landscape, the success of a business significantly hinges on its chosen model of operation. A business model isn't just about turning profits; it's a comprehensive framework that defines how a company creates, delivers, and captures value across different contexts. From direct consumer interactions to complex B2B environments, the right business model can dramatically affect the scalability, sustainability, and ultimate success of an organization.

Various business models exist from Business-to-Consumer (B2C) such as Freemium, Subscription, Marketplace, Direct Sales, Ad-based to Business-to-Business (B2B) such as SaaS, Licensing, White Label & Private Label, Supply Chain Management to Peer-to-Peer (P2P) such as P2P lending, Crowdsourcing, Blockchain-based to Hybrid Models such as Affiliate, Freeterprise, Transactional etc.

Revenue Streams: Clearly describe each revenue stream your company will utilize. For instance, if your business model includes direct sales (revenue generated from the direct sale of products or services to customers), subscription models (ongoing revenue generated from customers who pay a regular fee to access your product or service), licensing fees (Income derived from charging for the rights to use your intellectual property), freemium models (offer basic services for free while charging for premium features or enhancements) and advertising revenues (earnings accumulated from providing advertising space within your products or platforms), explain each.

Implementation and Contributions: Discuss how these revenue streams will be implemented and their expected contributions to the company's overall financial health. Detail the strategy for growing these streams over time and their potential impact on profitability.

Profitability Strategy:

Cost Structure and Pricing Strategy: Outline your startup's major cost areas and pricing strategy, explaining how they align with market expectations and how they compare to your competitors. Discuss strategic decisions that could enhance profitability, such as:

Partnerships: Establish collaborations or alliances that might lead to cost reductions or increased market reach.

Cost Savings: Implement measures to reduce costs, such as technology automation or outsourcing non-core activities.

Economies of Scale: Capitalize on benefits obtained from scaling up operations that reduce the cost per unit.

Competitive Pricing: Adopt a pricing strategy that is competitive yet profitable, based on thorough market research and competitor analysis.

Scalability:

Market Expansion: Explain how the business model facilitates expansion into new markets or regions without substantial increases in costs.

Product and Service Diversification: Discuss how the business could introduce new products or services, enhancing customer base and market share.

Targeting New Customer Segments: Detail strategies for reaching new customer demographics as the business grows, including marketing tactics and product adaptation.

Visual Elements:

Revenue Stream Charts: Use pie charts or bar graphs to visually break down the different revenue streams and their projected contributions to total revenue. This visual should help illustrate a diversified and stable revenue model.

Cost Structure Diagram: Provide a diagram that clearly shows how major cost areas relate to different parts of the business. Highlight any direct correlations between specific revenues and costs to show how profitability is managed.

Scalability Infographics: Develop an infographic that outlines potential growth paths for the business. This could include maps for geo expansion, timelines for product development, or diagrams showing the addition of new customer segments.

Conclusion and Transition:
Wrap up this slide by reinforcing how your business model is designed not only for current profitability but also for future growth. Transition smoothly into the next part of your pitch to build on the narrative of a robust and scalable business poised for success.

Slide 7: GTM Motion - Entering the Market

Purpose:
This slide is essential for detailing your strategy for market entry and expansion. It should outline the planned marketing and sales efforts that will drive customer acquisition, secure market share, and foster business growth.

Content:
Market Entry Strategy:
Geo Focus: Define the specific regions or countries where you plan to launch your products or services initially. Explain why these areas are targeted, based on market research, demand analysis, or competitive landscape.
Target Customer Segments: Identify and describe the key customer segments you aim to capture. Provide insights into their demographics, behaviors, and preferences to demonstrate understanding of your audience.
Phased Approaches or Pilot Programs: Discuss any staged rollout plans, such as starting with a pilot program to gather initial user feedback before a full-scale launch. Mention how these approaches will help refine your offerings and go-to-market tactics.

Marketing Tactics:

Digital Marketing:

SEO & SEM: Highlight strategies for improving organic search rankings and leveraging search marketing to drive targeted traffic.

Paid Social & Display Ads: Discuss targeted advertising campaigns on social media and across digital platforms to increase brand exposure and user acquisition.

Email Marketing: Emphasize personalized email campaigns to nurture leads, featuring segmentation, automated workflows, and conversion tracking.

Content Marketing & Branding:

Blogging & Video Content: Propose regular creation of engaging and informative content that addresses customer pain points and establishes thought leadership.

Webinars and Live Streams: Suggest organizing educational and interactive webinars or live streams to engage potential customers and promote products or services.

Public Relations & Media Outreach:

Press Releases & Media Kits: Discuss the use of press releases for major announcements and media kits that journalists can use to cover the brand.

Public Speaking & Panels: Consider participating in industry panels and speaking at conferences to build authority and visibility.

Influencer & Affiliate Marketing:

Influencer Collaborations: Detail plans for partnerships with influencers to leverage their audience for brand credibility and outreach.

Affiliate Programs: Suggest setting up an affiliate program that incentivizes others to promote your products in exchange for a commission.

Event Marketing & Sponsorships:

Trade Shows: Outline participation in trade shows to demonstrate products directly to potential customers and gather leads.

Sponsorships: Discuss sponsoring events or content in related industries to increase brand visibility among targeted demographics.

Sales Strategy:

Sales Channels & Distribution:

Direct Sales: Highlight the role of an in-house sales team in managing relationships and closing high-value deals.

Marketplace Platforms: Discuss using online marketplaces and e-commerce platforms to reach a wider audience.

Channel Partnerships: Suggest forming channel partnerships with other organizations to utilize their distribution networks for product sales.

Sales Team Development:

Recruitment & Training: Emphasize strategies for recruiting skilled sales personnel and providing ongoing training in sales techniques and product knowledge.

Performance Management: Outline methods for monitoring sales performance using KPIs and regular reviews to drive sales effectiveness.

Customer Relationship Management:

CRM Systems: Discuss the use of CRM systems to manage customer interactions and data to enhance customer relationships and retention.

Customer Feedback Loops: Consider implementing regular feedback channels to gather customer and prospect insights and inform sales strategies.

Innovative Sales Tactics & Technology:

AI and Machine Learning: Highlight the use of AI tools for predictive analytics to better understand customer behavior and optimize sales efforts.

Mobile Sales Tools: Consider the deployment of productivity tools that enable sales teams to manage leads and sales activities on the go.

Strategic Partnerships & Business Development:

Joint Ventures: Suggest exploring joint ventures with complementary businesses to co-develop products or enter new markets.

Cross-promotional Deals: Recommend developing cross-promotional deals with other companies to leverage each other's customer bases.

Visual Elements:

Entry Strategy Timeline: Create a timeline graphic showing the phased approach to market entry, marking significant milestones such as the launch in primary markets, assessment periods, and subsequent expansion phases.

Marketing Mix Diagram: Use diagrams or icons to represent various marketing tactics and how they integrate into your overall marketing strategy. This can visually depict the balance and focus across different channels and activities.

Sales Funnel Graphic: Design a visual representation of the sales funnel, showing the stages from lead generation through prospecting to closing deals. Highlight key actions or strategies applied at each stage to move prospects through the funnel.

Conclusion and Transition:

Conclude by emphasizing how your comprehensive GTM strategy is designed to effectively penetrate the market and achieve rapid growth. Transition to further reassure investors of your preparedness to execute the plan.

Slide 8: The Competition - Outlining the Battlefield

Purpose:
This slide is crucial for illustrating your understanding of the competitive landscape and articulating your startup's unique position within it. It aims to highlight your competitive advantages that differentiate your offering and outline strategic measures to maintain or enhance your market position.

Content:
Competitive Overview: Market Landscape: Provide an overview of the competitive landscape, identifying major players along with emerging

competitors. Mention market shares, established brand reputations, and any recent market entrants.

Potential Threats: Discuss potential threats in the market, including new technologies, regulatory changes, or shifts in consumer preferences that might impact competitive dynamics.

Differentiation:

Unique Features: Detail the unique features of your product or service that distinguish it from competitors. Whether it's an innovative use of technology, user experience enhancements, or unique service delivery methods, explain how these features provide added value to customers.

Performance and Quality: Highlight superior aspects of your offering such as better performance, higher quality, or reliability that have been acknowledged by customer feedback or comparative studies.

Cost Advantages: If applicable, discuss any cost advantages your product has over competitors, such as lower production costs, more efficient supply chain, or economies of scale.

Competitive Advantage:

Strategic Advantages: Elaborate on strategic advantages such as first-mover status, exclusive partnerships, or proprietary technologies that fortify your competitive position.

Sustainable Competitive Edge: Discuss how your competitive advantages are sustainable over the long term and how you plan to continue innovating and adapting.

SWOT Analysis:

Strengths: Identify key strengths that enhance your competitiveness (e.g., advanced R&D capabilities, strong leadership).

Weaknesses: Acknowledge internal weaknesses and outline plans to address them (e.g., limited marketing budget, dependency on supply chains).

Opportunities: Point out market opportunities that you are well-positioned to capitalize on (e.g., growing demand in an emerging market).
Threats: Identify external threats and your strategies for mitigating them (e.g., competitive responses, economic downturns).

Visual Elements:
Competitor Matrix: Construct a competitor matrix that compares your company against major competitors across various attributes such as price, features, market share, and customer satisfaction. This matrix should visually highlight where you excel.

SWOT Diagram: Present a well-organized SWOT analysis in a quadrant layout, making it visually easy for viewers to understand the strategic positioning.

Icons and Graphics: Use specific icons or graphics to symbolize your competitive strengths, like a shield for IP rights, a sprinter for quick market execution, or a brain for innovative solutions. These icons help convey complex ideas quickly and effectively.

Conclusion and Transition:
Conclude by reinforcing your strategic readiness to compete and excel in the marketplace. Transition into how your competitive positioning aligns with your long-term business strategies and growth plans.

Slide 9: Market Traction - Demonstrating Early Success

Purpose:
This slide is crucial for demonstrating the early successes of your product or service. It aims to instill confidence in investors by showing tangible proof of market acceptance and the potential for future growth.

Content:
Sales Figures:
Overview: Present clear and concise sales data or revenue growth figures that illustrate the market traction your product has gained.

Milestones: Highlight significant sales milestones, such as the first 1,000 customers, major contracts signed, or breakthroughs in new market segments.

Marquee Customers: If applicable, mention key customers or well-known companies that have adopted your solution, reinforcing credibility and market acceptance.

Customer Testimonials:

Credibility Through Satisfaction: Include compelling testimonials from satisfied customers. These should articulate the benefits and value derived from using your product or service, ideally addressing specific pain points or enhancements.

Diverse Voices: Try to showcase a range of testimonials from different customer segments or industries to demonstrate broad appeal and effectiveness.

Growth Metrics:

User Acquisition Rates: Discuss metrics such as the number of new users or customers over time, highlighting rapid adoption or steady growth patterns.

Retention Rates: Emphasize retention rates or repeat customer statistics, which are strong indicators of customer satisfaction and product stickiness.

Engagement Metrics: If relevant, include engagement metrics such as daily or monthly active users, session duration, or conversion rates that show how engaged users are with your product.

North Star Metric: A North Star Metric is the single metric that best captures the core value that your product delivers to customers. It is a key indicator of a company's success and is closely aligned with its growth and long-term goals. This metric often reflects the essence of what success means and is typically focused on customer or user engagement.

Examples of North Star Metrics of several popular companies are included in Appendix B.

Visual Elements:

Growth Charts: Employ line graphs or bar charts to visually represent the growth of sales, user numbers, or other key performance indicators over time. Ensure these charts are easy to read and clearly marked with important data points.

Customer Quotes: Design visually impactful graphics for customer testimonials. Use appealing fonts and colors to make these quotes stand out, ensuring they catch the viewer's attention and convey positive feedback effectively.

Metric Highlights: Utilize bullet points or small infographics to highlight essential growth metrics, such as user acquisition rates or retention percentages. Make sure to explain why these metrics are significant for assessing the health and potential of your business.

Conclusion and Transition:

Conclude by summarizing the proven market traction and the optimistic outlook it suggests for future growth. Transition smoothly into discussing moving forward with the confidence that the foundation of your business is solid and well-received in the market.

Slide 10: The Financials - Mapping the Numbers

Purpose:
The purpose of this slide is to provide a transparent overview of your financial status and projections, which are crucial for outlining the potential return on investment for potential investors. This ensures that stakeholders have a clear understanding of the financial health and strategic financial planning of your business.

Content:

Historical Financials:
Present key financials from previous years, including revenue, profit margins, and major expenses, to demonstrate your business's financial trajectory and health.

Highlight year-over-year growth rates and discuss any significant financial milestones or challenges and how they were managed.

Include EBITDA (Earnings Before Interest, Taxes, Depreciation, and Amortization) to provide insight into operational efficiency.

Projection Overview:
Share detailed financial projections for the next 3-5 years, including projected revenue, profits, and major expected expenses.

Break down revenue streams by product line or market segment to provide a deeper understanding of key drivers of growth.

Explain the assumptions behind your projections, such as market growth rates, pricing strategies, and expansion plans. Discuss both conservative and optimistic scenarios to illustrate potential risks and opportunities. Address how expected industry or economic changes might impact these projections.

Funding Use:
Clearly articulate how you plan to use the funds raised, linking budget allocations to specific growth initiatives such as market expansion, product development, or sales and marketing efforts.

Discuss expected outcomes from these investments, such as increased market share, improved profit margins, or faster scaling opportunities.

Provide a timeline for when these funds will be deployed, and when investors should expect to see measurable impacts on financials.

Visual Elements:

Financial Graphs:

Utilize line graphs or area charts to depict financial growth and projections clearly. These visuals should highlight trends in revenue growth, profit margins, and major expense categories.

Include comparative analysis if historical financials are available, showcasing the trajectory before and after key business decisions or market changes.

Funding Allocation Chart:

Create a pie chart or bar graph to visually represent how the raised funds will be allocated across different areas of the business such as R&D, marketing, capital expenditures, and new hires.

This visual should align with the narrative on how these allocations will drive growth and improve financial health.

Key Financial Metrics:

Highlight important financial metrics in a clear, visually engaging format. Metrics to include:

- **EBITDA** to indicate profitability and operating efficiency.
- **Customer Acquisition Cost (CAC) and Lifetime Value (LTV)** to show the effectiveness of marketing spend and long-term profitability per customer.
- **Burn Rate** to demonstrate cash flow and financial sustainability, especially important for startups or growth-phase businesses.
- For Subscription/SaaS companies, **Revenue Churn and Logo Churn** showcase retention scenarios.

Understanding these key financial metrics provides a comprehensive view of a company's financial health, operational efficiency, and long-term sustainability. These metrics are crucial for internal management decisions, external reporting, and they significantly influence investor decisions and company valuations.

Each metric offers a unique lens through which to view the financial implications of business strategies and market behaviors.

Use gauges, meter charts, or simple numeric displays to make these metrics easy to understand at a glance.

Benchmark Comparisons:

If applicable, include benchmark comparisons with industry averages or key competitors to contextualize your financial metrics. This comparison can help highlight your business's competitive advantages or areas for improvement.

Conclusion:

Wrap up by reiterating the strategic vision behind the financial projections and funding use, emphasizing how investor contributions will facilitate the next stages of growth and profitability. This conclusion should reinforce investor confidence in the scalability and financial acumen of your business strategy.

Slide 11: The Risks - Addressing Potential Hurdles

Purpose:
This slide aims to acknowledge and address potential risks and obstacles, demonstrating foresight and preparedness to potential investors. By clearly outlining identified risks and corresponding mitigation strategies, you convey a realistic understanding of the business environment and your capability to manage unforeseen challenges effectively.

Content:

Identified Risks:

Market Risks: Discuss risks such as changing market demands, economic downturns, or shifts in consumer preferences that could impact your business.

Technological Risks: Address potential challenges like technological obsolescence, cybersecurity threats, or technical failures that could disrupt operations.

Competitive Risks: Outline the threat posed by existing competitors or new entrants that could affect market share and profitability.

Regulatory Challenges: Highlight possible regulatory changes, compliance issues, or legal battles that could impose constraints on your business operations.

Mitigation Strategies:

Contingency Plans: Describe the specific actions your company would take in response to critical risks, such as alternative suppliers, backup systems, or emergency funding measures.

Insurance: Mention any relevant insurance policies that help mitigate financial risks associated with operational disruptions, legal liabilities, or property damages.

Strategic Partnerships: Explain how alliances with other companies or institutions can strengthen your market position, enhance technological capabilities, or improve regulatory compliance.

Ongoing Research and Development: Highlight your commitment to innovation as a way to stay ahead of technological risks and competitive pressures.

Resilience and Adaptability:

Provide examples of past instances where your company successfully navigated significant challenges or pivoted its strategy to adapt to new circumstances.

Emphasize the lessons learned from these experiences and how they have prepared your company to handle future risks more effectively.

Visual Elements:

Risk Matrix: Use a risk matrix to visually classify the potential impact (high, medium, low) and likelihood (likely, possible, unlikely) of each identified risk. This tool helps prioritize risk management efforts and provides a clear snapshot of the risk landscape for investors.

Flow Charts: Implement flow charts to demonstrate your mitigation processes or decision-making paths in response to potential risks. These charts should clearly show steps taken from the moment a risk is identified through to its resolution.

Icons: Utilize icons to symbolize different types of risks. For example:
A lightning bolt for operational risk, a gavel for legal/regulatory risk, a shield for security risk, a dollar sign in a downward arrow for financial risk.

Conclusion:

Conclude this slide by reassuring investors of your proactive approach to risk management. Emphasize that your strategic planning not only anticipates potential hurdles but also prepares robust measures to mitigate these risks effectively. This reassurance can significantly bolster investor confidence in the resilience and long-term stability of your business.

Slide 12: The Contingencies - Planning for Uncertainties

Purpose:

This slide is designed to demonstrate your company's strategic foresight by detailing how you prepare for unexpected market conditions or internal challenges. It reassures investors of your company's robustness and preparedness, enhancing confidence in its ability to sustain operations under various scenarios.

Content:

Scenario Planning:

Overview: Describe your approach to scenario planning, which involves preparing for multiple future conditions that could affect your business. This might include best-case, worst-case, and most likely scenarios.

Specific Scenarios: Outline plans for various potential future scenarios such as economic downturns, supply chain disruptions, sudden changes in consumer behavior, or technological advancements.

Action Plans: For each scenario, detail the specific strategies your company would employ to mitigate risks or capitalize on opportunities. This could involve diversifying supply chains, ramping up digital transformation, or shifting marketing strategies.

Emergency Fund:

Purpose and Size: Explain the rationale behind maintaining an emergency fund, such as protecting against cash flow interruptions or unforeseen expenses. Discuss the size of the fund relative to your operating expenses and how it's calculated based on risk assessments.

Management: Describe how this fund is managed, including investment strategies to preserve or grow its value while ensuring liquidity.

Flexible Operations:

Operational Flexibility: Discuss how your operational model is designed to allow flexibility and quick adaptation. This could include modular production systems, remote workforce capabilities, or scalable customer service solutions.

Real-Life Examples: Provide examples of past instances where your operational flexibility allowed you to quickly adapt to changing market dynamics or internal disruptions, underscoring the effectiveness of this approach.

Visual Elements:

Scenario Diagrams: Create diagrams that visually map out different scenarios and the corresponding action plans. These could be decision trees or flowcharts that guide the viewer through various paths depending on different conditions.

Budget Allocation Graphics: Show visually how much budget is allocated to contingency funds or emergency uses. Use pie charts or bar graphs to illustrate the percentage of total resources dedicated to these reserves, emphasizing prudent financial planning.

Flexibility Illustrations: Use simple graphics to represent the adaptability of your operations. Illustrations might include adjustable levers or fluid shapes that symbolize the ability to rapidly reconfigure operational processes. Other visuals could include interconnected nodes that demonstrate how different parts of your business can interact to support each other under stress.

Conclusion:

Conclude this slide by emphasizing that your proactive planning for various scenarios ensures the longevity and stability of your business. Highlight that these contingency plans are not merely reactive measures but are integral to your strategic operations, enhancing investor confidence in your management team's capacity to navigate future uncertainties effectively.

Slide 13: The Team - The Drivers of Success

Purpose:
This slide is crafted to introduce the core team behind the venture, emphasizing the expertise, experience, and commitment that are critical for achieving the startup's goals. It focuses particularly on the founders and key executives, showcasing the human capital poised to drive the company's success.

Content:

Founders:

Backgrounds and Inspirations: Detail the founders' professional backgrounds, educational achievements, and the experiences that inspired them to start the company. Highlight their industry expertise, previous entrepreneurial ventures, or key roles in relevant projects.

Reasons for Starting the Company: Explain the motivation behind the venture, such as addressing a significant market gap, a passion for innovation, or a desire to bring about social change.

Roles Within the Company: Describe how each founder's role is aligned with their skills and how they contribute to strategic decision-making and leadership.

Key Executives:
CEO (Chief Executive Officer): Describe the CEO's background, focusing on leadership experiences, industry knowledge, and previous successes in driving company vision and strategic direction.
COO (Chief Operating Officer): Highlight the COO's role in overseeing day-to-day administrative and operational functions, detailing experiences in streamlining operations for efficiency and effectiveness.
CFO (Chief Financial Officer): Outline the CFO's expertise in financial management, risk assessment, and budgeting, and their role in ensuring financial health and compliance.
CMO (Chief Marketing Officer): Discuss the CMO's experience in brand development, marketing strategies, and market research, which are vital for driving business growth and customer engagement.
CRO (Chief Revenue Officer): Explain the CRO's role in all revenue generation processes, focusing on their skills in sales leadership and revenue optimization across the company.
CTO (Chief Technology Officer): Provide insights into the CTO's technical background, innovations, and their role in product development and technology strategy.

Additional Key Individuals: Mention other critical personnel who play significant roles in the company's success, such as the head of HR or the Chief Strategy Officer, detailing their contributions to the company goals. Include other important roles as applicable, such as the Head of Product. Highlight the specific expertise these individuals bring to the team.

Team Dynamics:

Cultural Fit and Leadership: Discuss the leadership qualities and cultural fit among the team members that make your team uniquely capable of driving the company's success.

Shared Vision: Emphasize the unified vision of the team for the future of the company and their commitment to its long-term goals.

Training and Professional Development: Mention any ongoing training and development initiatives to enhance skills and adapt to evolving market demands.

Expansion Plans: Outline plans for expanding the team, especially if immediate hires are anticipated post-funding. Specify the roles you plan to fill and how these new members will help scale the business.

Visual Elements:

Team Photos: Include professional photos of the founders and key team members to personalize and foster a connection with the audience.

Skills Chart: Utilize a comprehensive chart to illustrate the diverse skills and areas of expertise across the team. This could highlight areas like leadership, innovation, market analysis, financial planning, and technological development.

Founders' Story Graphic: Create a visual narrative or timeline that encapsulates the founders' journey to starting the business, key milestones, and the evolution of their vision.

Growth Timeline:

Display a timeline showing the development of the team, noting significant additions over time and linking these to phases in the company's growth. Indicate future roles expected to be filled after funding.

Conclusion:

Conclude by affirming the team's robust combination of skills, visionary leadership, and proven track record, all of which fortify the company's capacity to navigate challenges and seize opportunities. Emphasize that this strong foundation not only enhances the company's ability to achieve its current objectives but also equips it to scale and adapt to future demands, bolstering investor confidence in the team's ability to execute the business strategy effectively.

Slide 14: Target Milestones - Setting the Roadmap

Purpose:

This slide is designed to outline the strategic roadmap and key milestones that your startup aims to achieve, demonstrating your planned path for growth and the strategic objectives that will guide your progress. It serves to give investors a clear vision of your company's future direction and the steps you are taking to get there.

Content:

Milestone Overview:
Product Development Milestones: Detail the critical phases of product development, such as prototype completion, beta testing, and full-scale launch.
Market Entry Points: Outline when and how you plan to enter new markets, including geographic expansions or targeting new customer segments.
Customer Acquisition Targets: Set specific goals for customer growth, such as reaching numbers of users or achieving market penetration rates.

Operational Achievements: Describe significant operational improvements you aim to achieve, such as establishing key partnerships, optimizing the supply chain, or implementing new production technologies.

Timeline:

Provide a chronological timeline that places these milestones in the order they are expected to be achieved. This timeline should span the short to medium term, typically covering the next 1-5 years. Ensure the timeline reflects realistic expectations and aligns with your overall business strategy and financial projections.

Impact of Milestones:

Explain how achieving each milestone will impact the business. For instance, discuss how product development milestones will enhance your product offering and appeal to a broader customer base. Describe how market entry and customer acquisition milestones will increase market share and contribute to revenue growth. Highlight how operational milestones will enhance efficiency, reduce costs, or improve product quality.

Visual Elements:

Interactive Timeline:

Design an interactive or visually engaging timeline that is easy to follow. Each milestone could be represented with a brief description or an icon that summarizes the milestone's focus. Consider using tools or digital platforms that allow viewers to interact with the timeline, such as clicking on milestones to reveal more detailed information.

Impact Icons:

Use distinct icons next to each milestone to visually represent the type of impact or benefit. For example, use a dollar sign for revenue increases, a globe for market expansion, or a gear for technology upgrades. These icons help quickly convey the significance of each milestone at a glance, making the slide more engaging and informative.

Progress Indicators:

If applicable, include visual progress indicators that show the current status of each milestone. This could be a simple progress bar or a color-coded system indicating not started, in progress, and completed. These indicators provide a dynamic snapshot of where the company currently stands in its roadmap, offering a real-time look at achievements and forthcoming objectives.

Conclusion:

Conclude by emphasizing that the outlined milestones are pivotal for steering the company towards its strategic goals. Reinforce that these planned achievements are grounded in careful planning and robust market analysis, ensuring that they are both achievable and impactful. This slide should leave investors with a clear understanding of how your company plans to grow, innovate, and succeed in the coming years.

Slide 15: The Ask - Securing Strategic Investment

Purpose:

This slide is designed to clearly articulate your funding requirements, outlining how much capital is needed, what it will be used for, and the expected outcomes or returns that these investments will facilitate. It is critical to include this slide as it provides a direct call-to-action for investors and efficiently drives the next step in the investment process.

Content:

Funding Requirements:
Total Amount Needed: Specify the exact amount of funding you are seeking. If your funding needs are staggered, outline the stages or rounds of funding and the amounts needed at each stage.

Timing: Explain the timeline for the funding needs, indicating when each tranche of funds will be required and what milestones are expected to be achieved with each funding stage.

Use of Funds:

Detailed Allocation: Break down how the funds will be allocated across different areas such as product development, marketing, staff expansion, infrastructure, etc. Be specific to show thoughtful planning and demonstrate your financial acumen.

Justification for Each Allocation: For each area of fund allocation, provide a rationale on how this expenditure will contribute to business growth and enhance operational capabilities.

Expected Returns:

Equity Value Projections: Provide an overview of what investors can expect in return for their investment in terms of equity value increase.

Exit Strategies: Outline potential exit strategies for investors, such as an IPO, acquisition, or buyback options. Include examples of exits via IPO or M&A of similar companies to further substantiate your point of view.

Other Financial Returns: Discuss other potential financial returns, such as dividends or profit sharing, if applicable.

Visual Elements:

Funding Graphs: Use clear and straightforward graphs to depict the stages of funding and the amounts required at each stage. This visual representation helps investors quickly grasp the financial trajectory and funding lifecycle of your startup.

Budget Allocation Chart: Create a detailed pie chart or bar graph showing how the funds will be allocated. This chart should visually break down the budget, providing transparency and reinforcing the strategic planning behind the proposed spending.

Return Projections: Include visuals such as line graphs or projection tables that illustrate potential financial returns or growth in valuation. These visuals help paint a compelling picture of the investment's potential, making the opportunity tangible and enticing for investors.

Note: Including a slide on "The Ask" is crucial in a pitch deck, yet it is often overlooked. While many pitches successfully highlight the technology, they often fail to directly address why an investor should buy equity in the company. This slide is one of the most important as it not only provides a strong call-to-action but also clearly sets the stage for what you expect from investors and what they can expect in return. It efficiently moves the conversation towards securing the investment and establishes a clear path forward.

Conclusion:

Conclude by emphasizing the strategic importance of the investment for both the startup and the potential investors. Reaffirm that the requested funding aligns with well-defined milestones and objectives that will drive significant growth and enhance shareholder value. Invite investors to engage in further discussions to explore the details and potential of the investment, prompting an immediate and clear next step in the investment process.

CHAPTER 7: HANDLING QUESTIONS AND OBJECTIONS

"Anticipating and addressing questions and objections with confidence transforms potential challenges into opportunities to reinforce your pitch, demonstrating preparedness and resilience to investors."

Section 1: Preparing for Common Questions and Challenges from Investors

Engaging with potential investors extends beyond delivering a compelling pitch deck. The Q&A session that follows is a critical component of the investment process, where investors scrutinize the potential of your business.

Business Model and Strategy: Investors may ask about the sustainability of your business model, your competitive advantage, and how you plan to scale. Be ready to discuss the unique aspects of your model, any proprietary technology or processes, and your long-term strategy for growth and market domination.

Market Analysis: Expect questions about the size of your target market, growth potential, and your market penetration strategy. Prepare to provide data on market research, customer demographics, and case studies or testimonials that demonstrate demand for your product or service.

Financial Projections: Detailed inquiries about your financial projections, including revenue streams, cost structure, and profitability timelines, are common. Have clear, realistic financial models ready to show, with explanations for your assumptions and scenarios for best and worst-case projections.

Team Capabilities: Investors often probe the competence and experience of your team. Be prepared to highlight the team's background, previous successes, and specific skills that contribute to the potential success of your venture.

Prepared Responses:

Data-Backed: Ensure that your responses are supported with data. This could include market statistics, financial figures, or user metrics that substantiate your business case.

Conciseness: While detail is important, your answers should be concise and to the point. Practice delivering key points succinctly to maintain investor interest and focus.

Value Reinforcement: Each answer should reinforce your business's value proposition. Connect your responses back to the core strengths of your business and how it aligns with investor interests and market demands.

Mock Sessions:

Regular Practice: Conduct regular mock Q&A sessions with various stakeholders such as mentors, advisors, or team members. This will help you handle different types of questions and adjust your responses accordingly.

Feedback Utilization: Use feedback from these sessions to refine your answers, improve your delivery, and build confidence. Pay attention to both content and presentation; how you say something can be as important as what you say.

Stress Testing: Include sessions that simulate high-pressure situations to prepare you for tough questions and to improve your composure under stress. This is particularly useful for handling unexpected or difficult questions effectively.

Additional Tips

Storytelling: Where applicable, use storytelling to make your answers more engaging and memorable. This can help illustrate points more clearly and make technical information more accessible.

Anticipate Challenges: Beyond questions, be prepared for potential skepticism or challenges to your business model or projections. Have a rationale ready for why things will work, backed by research or examples.

Understanding Investor Motivations: Tailor your responses based on the specific interests or focus areas of the investors you are pitching to. Understanding their portfolio, investment thesis, and previous investments can provide valuable clues to the type of questions they might ask.

Conclusion

Preparation for the investor Q&A session is crucial and can dictate the success of your fundraising efforts. By anticipating questions, refining your responses, and practicing your delivery, you can engage more effectively with potential investors and significantly improve your chances of securing the investment you need. This preparation not only shows professionalism but also a deep understanding of your business and market, instilling greater confidence in potential investors.

Section 2: Crafting an Elevator Pitch

An elevator pitch is an essential tool for any entrepreneur, providing a quick and compelling overview of your business to spark interest and open doors for deeper conversations. Here's how to craft an effective elevator pitch:

Core Components of an Elevator Pitch

Startup's Name: Start with the name of your company to establish identity.
The Problem You Solve: Define the problem in the market that your startup addresses. This sets the context for the value of your solution.
Your Solution: Describe what your startup does or what product/service it offers to solve the identified problem.
Unique Value Proposition (UVP): Highlight what makes your solution unique or superior to existing alternatives. This could be your technology, methodology, or business model.

Market Opportunity: Briefly mention the market you are targeting and its potential size to underscore the growth opportunity.

Conciseness and Clarity

Duration: Keep your pitch concise, aiming for 30 seconds or less. This ensures you can deliver it in a brief elevator ride or a quick hallway conversation.
Language: Use clear, simple language that avoids jargon. The goal is to be understood by someone not familiar with your industry or technology.
Focus: Concentrate on the most compelling aspects of your business. What would matter most to someone hearing about your company for the first time?

Practice

Repetition: Practice your pitch repeatedly until it becomes second nature. This helps in delivering it smoothly under pressure.
Adaptation: Prepare to slightly tweak your pitch depending on the audience or scenario. What you emphasize might change based on the interests or background of the listener.
Feedback: Try your pitch on trusted colleagues or mentors and refine it based on their feedback.

Template for an Elevator Pitch

Here is a simple template you can adapt and use:

"[Company] is creating [Specified Offering] aimed at supporting [Audience] in addressing [Challenge] through [Innovative Approach]. Setting ourselves apart from [Competitor 1] and [Competitor 2], our strategy includes [Uniqueness]. We are engaging with the [Targeted Market] market, which is worth [Market Valuation]. Currently, our [Status of Product /Company/ Team] is [Description], and we are seeking [Funding] to [Purpose]."

Your elevator pitch should be compelling, concise, and clear, with a focus on what sets your business apart and why it matters. Practice delivering your pitch to ensure you are always ready to make a great first impression.

Section 3: Using Backup Slides Effectively

Backup slides are an essential part of your presentation toolkit, particularly during investor meetings where detailed questions are likely to arise. They are not shown in the main presentation but are kept ready for use during the Q&A session to provide in-depth information and support your responses with data and visuals.

Content of Backup Slides

Technical Specifications: Prepare slides that offer detailed insights into the technology behind your product, such as architecture diagrams, technology stacks, or patent information. This can be crucial for tech-oriented investors or those interested in the innovative aspects of your product.

Financial Breakdowns: Include detailed financial data such as monthly burn rate, detailed cost structure, historical financial performance, and revenue projections with underlying assumptions. This could also include sensitivity analyses or scenario planning.

Extended Market Analysis: Provide deeper insights into the market with slides on competitive analysis, market segmentation, customer demographics, and go-to-market strategy. This could also include results from customer surveys or case studies that validate market demand.

Operational Details:

Supply Chain Information: For businesses that rely heavily on manufacturing or product distribution, detailed slides on your supply chain, logistics model, and vendor relationships can be important.

Regulatory Compliance: If applicable, include information on regulatory approvals, compliance measures, and any legal considerations that impact your business.

Organization and Accessibility

Logical Order: Organize your backup slides in a logical sequence that follows the flow of the main presentation. This makes it easier to find the right slide during the heat of a Q&A session.

Segmentation: Group slides into categories such as "Financials," "Technology," "Market Analysis," and "Regulations." This categorization helps in quickly navigating to the relevant section during discussions.

Familiarity with Content:

Practice Sessions: Regularly review and practice with your backup slides. Being familiar with the content allows you to quickly recall and present the relevant slide without appearing unprepared or hesitant.

Cue Cards or Notes: Consider having cue cards or brief notes that summarize the key points of each backup slide. This can help in swiftly pulling up the necessary information without going through multiple slides during the presentation.

Integration into the Q&A

Proactive Use: Don't wait for a question to arise; if you feel a slide can effectively add value to an answer or pre-empt a potential question, proactively introduce the slide during your response.
Visual Support: Use visuals such as charts, graphs, and diagrams extensively in your backup slides. Visual data can be more impactful in conveying complex information quickly and clearly.

Conclusion

Backup slides are your secret weapon during investor presentations, especially during the Q&A. They should be detailed, well-organized, and ready at your fingertips to address specific questions or concerns from investors.

By effectively preparing and utilizing these slides, you demonstrate thorough preparation, transparency, and professionalism, significantly enhancing the credibility of your pitch and the confidence of potential investors in your business.

Section 4: Tips on Engaging Confidently and Effectively with VCs

Engaging with VCs is a crucial skill for entrepreneurs seeking investment. It requires not just a deep understanding of your own business, but also an appreciation of the VC's perspective and expectations. Effective engagement can greatly enhance your chances of securing funding.

Understanding the Investor's Perspective

Research Backgrounds: Before meeting with a VC, research their background, including their investment history, areas of interest, and industry expertise. This will help you tailor your pitch to resonate with their specific preferences and strategic focus.

Identify Investment Philosophy: Understanding whether a VC is risk-averse or risk-tolerant, or if they prefer early-stage startups or more mature companies, can shape the way you present your business model and growth potential.

Review Portfolio: Look at other companies the VC has invested in. This provides insights into the kinds of businesses they find attractive, and potential synergies or conflicts within their portfolio that could influence their decision to invest in your startup.

Body Language and Tone

Eye Contact: Maintain steady eye contact to convey confidence and sincerity. This non-verbal cue is essential in building trust and rapport.

Open Gestures: Use open gestures to communicate your enthusiasm and openness. Avoid crossing your arms or other closed body language that might suggest defensiveness or discomfort.

Confident Tone: Speak clearly and assertively to demonstrate your command of the subject matter. However, balance this by not coming across as arrogant or dismissive of alternative viewpoints.

Listening Skills

Active Engagement: Show active listening by nodding in agreement where appropriate, and acknowledging the points raised by investors.

Clarify Questions: If a question is unclear, don't hesitate to ask for clarification. This shows that you are attentive and committed to providing thoughtful answers.

Honest Responses: If you don't know the answer to a question, admit it openly but assure the VC that you will get back to them with the information. This honesty can build credibility and trust.

Visual Elements

FAQ Sheets: Prepare a visual FAQ sheet that summarizes common Q&A about your business. This can be shared with investors after your pitch to reinforce key points and provide additional clarity.

Flow Charts for Backup Slides: Create flow charts that help you navigate your backup slides efficiently. This tool will ensure you can quickly find the right information during a Q&A session.

Tips Sheet: Develop a concise tips sheet for engaging with VCs that you and your team can refer to. This should include key points on communication style, common questions to prepare for, and reminders about investor engagement.

Conclusion

Successfully engaging with VCs involves more than just knowing your business; it requires strategic preparation and understanding how to communicate effectively. By anticipating questions, presenting confidently, and responding thoughtfully, you demonstrate not only your business acumen but also your ability to navigate the complexities of investor relationships.

CHAPTER 8: AFTER THE PITCH

"The journey doesn't end after the pitch; it's where the real work begins. Following up with persistence, addressing feedback, and nurturing investor relationships are key steps to turning a promising pitch into a successful partnership."

Steps to Follow Post-Pitch

Securing venture capital is a continuous process that extends well beyond the initial pitch. The actions you take after your presentation are crucial in maintaining the interest of potential investors and can significantly influence the outcome of your fundraising efforts. Here's what you should focus on:

Solicit Feedback:

Immediate Request: Ask for feedback directly after your presentation. This can be done in a respectful and constructive manner, showing that you value the investors' insights.

Specific Questions: Pose specific questions about what investors thought were the strengths and weaknesses of your pitch. Ask about both the presentation style and the content, particularly your business model and the opportunity you are presenting.

Reflect and Refine:

Incorporate Changes: Use the feedback to refine your pitch. If certain aspects of your business model or financial projections were unclear or unconvincing, consider how you can adjust these sections.

Address Concerns: Directly address any specific concerns that were raised. If investors questioned the scalability of your business, for example, you might need to provide more evidence or refine your strategy to better articulate how you plan to grow.

Follow-Up

Immediate Thank You: Send a thank you note to all the investors who attended your pitch within 24 hours. Express your appreciation for their time and consideration.

Detailed Responses: If there were questions you couldn't answer during the pitch, follow up with detailed responses after the meeting. This not only shows that you are thorough but also that you are committed to transparency and open communication.

Regular Updates: Even if investors initially decide not to proceed, keep them updated on your progress. Regular updates can keep your startup top of mind and may lead to investment at a later stage.

Building Relationships

Networking: Continue to engage with the venture capital community. Attend networking events, participate in forums, and stay active in the startup ecosystem. Building relationships can open doors to other funding opportunities, partnerships, and valuable advice.

Seek Advice: Don't hesitate to ask for advice from investors, even if they chose not to invest. Many investors are willing to provide guidance and mentorship to promising entrepreneurs, and this can sometimes lead to an investment in the future.

Leveraging Investor Connections

Introductions: Ask investors whether they can introduce you to other potential investors or strategic partners. Even if they aren't interested in investing, they might see potential in your idea and be willing to help you.

Collaborations: Look for opportunities to collaborate with other companies in the investors' portfolios. This can provide mutual benefits and may increase your attractiveness as an investment.

Not All Pitches Result in Investments

While pitching to investors is a critical step for securing funding, it does not always guarantee an investment. There are several reasons why investors might decide to pass on an opportunity. Some of these include:

- It's Too Early
- No Niche Understanding
- Portfolio Overlap
- Concerns About Your Team
- No Business Plan
- Lack of Trust in Your Idea
- No Scalable GTM Channels
- Ignorance of KPIs
- Failing to Understand Competition
- Short Runway
- No Skin in the Game

You will find more details on each of these in Appendix C.

It's crucial not to feel disheartened and to adhere to the post-pitch guidelines detailed in this section.

Often, a "no" doesn't signify "never," but rather just "not now."

CHAPTER 9: TOP DO'S AND DONT'S TO ACE YOUR PITCH

"A successful pitch is crafted through clarity, confidence, and connection. Master the do's and avoid the don'ts to leave a lasting impression and drive your vision home with investors."

Top 25 Do's

- **Start Strong**: Open with a powerful statement that hooks your investor audience.
- **Know Your Audience**: Tailor your pitch to the interests and backgrounds of the investors.
- **Tell a Story**: Use storytelling to make your pitch memorable and engaging.
- **Show Passion**: Convey enthusiasm and belief in your project.
- **Be Concise**: Keep your presentation brief and to the point.
- **Focus on the Problem**: Clearly articulate the problem you are solving.
- **Highlight Your Solution**: Clearly explain how your product or service solves the problem.
- **Demonstrate Market Fit**: Provide evidence of market demand and your product's fit.
- **Use Data Effectively**: Support your arguments with relevant and convincing data.
- **Showcase Your Team**: Highlight the experience and skills of your team members.
- **Understand Your Competition**: Clearly identify your competitors and your advantages over them.
- **Detail Your Business Model**: Explain how you will make money.
- **Discuss Financials**: Include detailed financial projections and funding needs.
- **Explain Your Funding Use**: Articulate how the investment will be used.
- **Be Realistic**: Keep financial projections, timelines, and growth expectations realistic.
- **Prepare for Questions**: Anticipate potential investor questions and prepare clear, concise responses.

- **Practice Your Pitch**: Rehearse your presentation multiple times to ensure smooth delivery.
- **Use Visual Aids**: Enhance your pitch with professional, clear visual aids.
- **Show Traction**: Provide evidence of early success or market traction.
- **Address Risks**: Acknowledge potential risks and your strategies for mitigating them.
- **Be Transparent**: Be honest about challenges and setbacks.
- **Show Scalability**: Demonstrate the potential for growth and scalability of your business.
- **Follow Up:** Send thank-you notes and respond promptly to follow-up questions.
- **Seek Feedback**: After pitches, ask for feedback to improve future presentations.
- **Continuously Improve**: Refine your pitch based on feedback and changing market conditions.

Top 25 Don'ts

- **Avoid Jargon**: Don't use overly technical language or acronyms that might confuse the audience.
- **Don't Overload Slides**: Avoid cluttering your slides with too much information.
- **Don't Underestimate the Competition**: Never dismiss or underestimate your competitors.
- **Avoid Unclear Financials**: Don't provide vague or overly optimistic financial forecasts without justification.
- **Don't Skip the 'Ask'**: Clearly state how much money you are raising and the terms.
- **Don't Ignore Market Size**: Avoid neglecting details about the market size and growth potential.
- **Don't Be Rigid**: Don't come off as inflexible or unwilling to adapt your business model.
- **Avoid Misleading Statements**: Never make false or unverifiable claims about your product or market.

- **Don't Forget the Exit Strategy**: Avoid leaving out potential exit strategies for investors.
- **Don't Be Overly Technical**: Avoid deep technical dives unless specifically asked.
- **Don't Disregard Design**: Avoid poor or inconsistent visual design in your pitch deck.
- **Don't Speak Monotonously**: Avoid a dull, monotonous presentation style.
- **Don't Ignore Questions**: Never dismiss or trivialize investor questions.
- **Avoid Lack of Preparation**: Don't come unprepared to answer common investor queries.
- **Don't Overlook Your Unique Selling Proposition (USP)**: Always highlight what sets your business apart.
- **Don't Ignore Your Team**: Don't fail to mention the team behind your project and their credentials.
- **Avoid Negative Attitudes**: Don't express negativity about challenges or past failures.
- **Don't Lack a Backup Plan**: Avoid having no contingency plans for potential obstacles.
- **Don't Be Impersonal**: Avoid a lack of personal connection or engagement with the audience.
- **Don't Rush**: Avoid rushing through your presentation.
- **Don't Be Defensive**: Avoid reacting defensively to feedback or challenging questions.
- **Avoid Poor Timing**: Don't mismanage your allotted time; keep track and pace your presentation.
- **Don't Forget to Network**: Don't miss the opportunity to network before and after the pitch.
- **Don't Leave Out Details on Scalability**: Avoid vague statements about how your business will scale.
- **Don't Neglect Post-Pitch Engagement**: Don't fail to follow up or keep potential investors engaged after the pitch.

By following these do's and avoiding the don'ts, you can create a strong, effective pitch that resonates with venture capitalists and maximizes your chances of securing funding.

CHAPTER 10: ESSENTIAL CHECKLIST TO ACE YOUR PITCH

"Thorough preparation is the cornerstone of a winning pitch. Use this checklist to ensure every detail is perfected, transforming your presentation into a compelling and convincing narrative."

Pre-Pitch Preparation

Research Your Audience: Understand the backgrounds, focus areas, and investment history of your potential investors to tailor your pitch effectively.

Define Your Value Proposition: Clearly articulate what your company does, the unique problem it solves, and why it's relevant now.

Design Your Pitch Deck: Ensure your pitch deck is visually appealing with a consistent design theme, high-quality graphics, and a clear flow.

Craft a Compelling Narrative: Tell a story that logically connects the problem, your solution, the market opportunity, and your execution strategy.

Refine Your Elevator Pitch: Develop a succinct description of your business that encapsulates the essence of your value proposition in 30 seconds.

Building the Pitch Deck

Slide 1 - The Problem:
Content: Introduce the market gap or specific problem your startup addresses. Use compelling data or anecdotes to underscore the necessity of your solution.
Purpose: Set the stage by highlighting the problem to establish the need for your solution.

Slide 2 - Market Validation:
Content: Provide robust market research data, industry size, growth rate, and analysis that supports the demand for your solution.
Purpose: Demonstrate that there is a significant, addressable market that needs your solution.

Slide 3 - The Solution:
Content: Describe how your product or service solves the problem identified. Include unique features and benefits.
Purpose: Clearly showcase your solution's value proposition and how it differs from existing alternatives.

Slide 4 - The Company:
Content: Outline your company's mission, vision, and core values. Show how these align with market needs and opportunities.
Purpose: Establish the ethos of your company, and how it's uniquely positioned to execute the solution.

Slide 5 - Technology & IP:
Content: Discuss technological innovations, intellectual property, patents held, and how these contribute to your competitive edge.
Purpose: Highlight your tech expertise and proprietary technologies that protect your market position.

Slide 6 - Business Model:
Content: Detail how your business will generate revenue. Explain your pricing strategy, customer segments, revenue streams, and scalability.
Purpose: Show investors how your company makes money and plans to grow financially.

Slide 7 - GTM Strategy:
Content: Present your go-to-market strategy, detailing marketing and sales tactics, and expected pathways to capture market share.
Purpose: Outline your approach to entering the market and how you will acquire and grow your customer base.

Slide 8 - The Competition:
Content: Provide a competitive analysis, identifying key competitors and your strategic advantages. Include a SWOT analysis if relevant.
Purpose: Convey a clear understanding of the competitive landscape and why your solution is superior.

Slide 9 - Market Traction:
Content: Show early success, key metrics, growth indicators, and customer testimonials to demonstrate market acceptance.
Purpose: Provide proof of concept and evidence that the market responds positively to your product or service.

Slide 10 - The Financials:
Content: Present detailed financial projections, key metrics like CAC, LTV, burn rate, and your funding needs.
Purpose: Provide a clear picture of financial health, future financial planning, and investment requirements.

Slide 11 - The Risks:
Content: Identify potential risks and your strategies for mitigating them.
Purpose: Show investors that you are realistic and prepared to handle challenges.

Slide 12 - The Contingencies:
Content: Detail plans for handling unexpected market changes or challenges.
Purpose: Demonstrate foresight and strategic planning in unpredictable situations.

Slide 13 - The Team:
Content: Introduce key team members, their backgrounds, key experiences, and specific roles.
Purpose: Highlight the capability and expertise of your team to execute the business plan.

Slide 14 - Target Milestones:
Content: Outline strategic objectives, key milestones for the next phases, including product development, market expansion, etc.
Purpose: Show the roadmap and key goals that will guide your company's growth trajectory.

Slide 15 - The Ask:
Content: Clearly specify the amount of funding you are seeking, how it will be used, and the expected impact on your company.
Purpose: Conclude with a clear call to action for investment, outlining the terms and potential returns for investors.

Practice and Refinement

Rehearse Your Pitch: Practice your delivery to ensure clarity, confidence, and timing.

Gather Feedback: Present to peers or mentors and refine your pitch based on their constructive criticism.

Anticipate Investor Questions: Prepare clear and concise responses for potential questions about your business model, market, and financials.

Day of the Pitch

Final Review: Double-check your pitch deck for any errors and ensure all data is up-to-date.

Check All Equipment: Verify that presentation tools and technology are functioning correctly to avoid any technical difficulties.

Dress Professionally: Wear appropriate attire that aligns with the expectations of your audience.

Engaging with Investors

Deliver with Confidence and Clarity: Engage your audience with a clear, passionate presentation and maintain eye contact.

Responsive Q&A: Handle questions with poise, demonstrating depth of knowledge and readiness to adapt.

Effective Follow-Up: Send a thoughtful thank-you note summarizing key points and expressing enthusiasm for a partnership.

Post-Pitch Engagement

Keep the Dialogue Going: Provide regular updates on your progress to keep interested investors engaged and informed.

Incorporate Feedback: Continuously refine your pitch and business model based on investor feedback to improve for future presentations.

Prepare for Further Discussions: Anticipate and prepare for deeper due diligence, further discussions, and potential investment negotiations.

CASE STUDIES

"Learning from real-world successes and challenges provides invaluable insights. These case studies illustrate the nuanced strategies and tactics that can turn a pitch into a triumph."

I. Case Study: Square

https://tinyurl.com/square-casestudy

Square's pitch deck for their early funding rounds provides an insightful look into how they positioned themselves to potential investors as a transformative player in the mobile payments space. Square sought to revolutionize the way small businesses and individuals process payments by offering an intuitive, affordable, and efficient solution.

This case study compares Square's pitch deck to the structured guidelines provided in "Ace the Pitch," evaluating how well the deck adheres to the recommended format for maximum impact.

This analysis examines each component of Square's presentation, from identifying market gaps to detailing financial projections and risks.

The goal is to provide a comprehensive evaluation that can serve as a guide for entrepreneurs on how to craft compelling, investor-ready pitch decks that clearly communicate their value propositions and business strategies.

Slide 1: The Problem - Unveiling Market Gaps

- Square Pitch Deck: Identifies the issues with traditional card readers being unwieldy and expensive, and the difficulty for small business owners to use card services.
- "Ace the Pitch" Approach: Clearly outlines a significant problem in the market, setting a strong foundation for introducing Square's solution.

Slide 2: Market Validation - Confirming the Demand

- Square Pitch Deck: Demonstrates the rapidly growing mobile payments market and the increasing interest in mobile payments solutions.
- "Ace the Pitch" Approach: Provides solid data to validate the market demand, aligning well with this guideline.

Slide 3: The Solution - Bridging the Gap

- Square Pitch Deck: Presents Square as an easy-to-adopt platform that satisfies both buyers and vendors through a simple, intuitive process.
- "Ace the Pitch" Approach: Clearly describes how Square's solution addresses the identified problems, bridging the market gap effectively.

Slide 4: The Company - Vision and Mission

- Square Pitch Deck: Discusses the team's vision to create a zero-friction, efficient payment solution, emphasizing simplicity and efficiency.
- "Ace the Pitch" Approach: Effectively communicates the company's vision and mission, guiding its strategic objectives.

Slide 5: Technology & IP - Securing the Edge

- Square Pitch Deck: Describes the technology behind Square, including the card reader, data conversion, and secure transaction processing.
- "Ace the Pitch" Approach: Highlights the unique technological innovations and intellectual property that provide Square a competitive edge.

Slide 6: Business Model - Sustaining Value Creation

- Square Pitch Deck: Explains the revenue model, including a flat 2.75% fee per swipe and no additional fees.
- "Ace the Pitch" Approach: Clearly outlines how Square generates revenue and sustains its business model.

Slide 7: GTM Motion - Entering the Market

- Square Pitch Deck: Discusses customer acquisition strategies, targeting small businesses and individuals, with a focus on social media, internet advertising, and partnerships.
- "Ace the Pitch" Approach: Provides an overview of the go-to-market strategy, though more detail on specific tactics would enhance this section.

Slide 8: The Competition - Outlining the Battlefield

- Square Pitch Deck: Lists direct competitors and highlights Square's advantages such as no credit checks, no monthly fees, and device compatibility.
- "Ace the Pitch" Approach: Effectively outlines the competitive landscape and Square's differentiators.

Slide 9: Market Traction - Demonstrating Early Success

- Square Pitch Deck: Shows traction through metrics like customer growth, number of payments processed, and partnerships.
- "Ace the Pitch" Approach: Successfully demonstrates early market traction with concrete data, building investor confidence.

Slide 10: The Financials - Mapping the Numbers

- Square Pitch Deck: Provides financial projections, revenue growth, and EBITDA margins.
- "Ace the Pitch" Approach: Detailed financials are included, though more historical financial data would further strengthen this section.

Slide 11: The Risks - Addressing Potential Hurdles

- Square Pitch Deck: Lists potential concerns such as NFC technology overtaking credit card usage and execution risks.
- "Ace the Pitch" Approach: Addresses potential risks and provides responses, aligning well with this guideline.

Slide 12: The Contingencies - Planning for Uncertainties

- Square Pitch Deck: Does not explicitly discuss contingencies.
- "Ace the Pitch" Approach: Would benefit from discussing contingency plans for unexpected market or operational challenges.

Slide 13: The Team - The Drivers of Success

- Square Pitch Deck: Introduces the management team, highlighting their backgrounds and relevant experiences.
- "Ace the Pitch" Approach: Effectively showcases the team, enhancing investor confidence in their capability to execute the business plan.

Slide 14: Target Milestones - Setting the Roadmap

- Square Pitch Deck: Lists future financial projections and growth assumptions but lacks specific milestones.
- "Ace the Pitch" Approach: Would benefit from a more detailed roadmap with specific, time-bound milestones for future development.

Slide 15: The Ask - Securing Strategic Investment

- Square Pitch Deck: Specifies the investment needed, expected IRR, and potential exit strategies.
- "Ace the Pitch" Approach: Clearly states the investment ask and how it will be used, aligning well with best practices.

II. Case Study: Buffer

https://tinyurl.com/buffer-casestudy

Buffer's seed round pitch deck offers a compelling case study of how to effectively communicate a startup's value proposition to potential investors. Buffer, a platform designed to streamline social media scheduling and analytics, presents a detailed narrative of its market opportunity, solution, and business model. This case study rigorously compares Buffer's pitch deck to the structured guidelines outlined in "Ace the Pitch," providing a comprehensive evaluation of how well Buffer adheres to the recommended pitch structure.

Slide 1: The Problem - Unveiling Market Gaps

- Buffer Pitch Deck: Identifies inefficiencies in social media management, particularly the challenges of scheduling and managing posts across different platforms.
- "Ace the Pitch" Approach: Effectively defines the problem, setting the stage for introducing Buffer's solution.

Slide 2: Market Validation - Confirming the Demand

- Buffer Pitch Deck: Cites social media usage trends and the increasing importance of social media marketing, backed by statistics like the daily number of tweets and Facebook shares.
- "Ace the Pitch" Approach: Uses solid market data to confirm the growing demand for social media management tools, aligning well with the guidelines.

Slide 3: The Solution - Bridging the Gap

- Buffer Pitch Deck: Presents Buffer as a solution that simplifies social media management through easy scheduling and analytics, aiming to improve efficiency and effectiveness for users.
- "Ace the Pitch" Approach: Clearly articulates how Buffer's features address the problems identified, effectively bridging the identified market gaps.

Slide 4: The Company - Vision and Mission

- Buffer Pitch Deck: This aspect is not explicitly covered in the provided slides.
- "Ace the Pitch" Approach: Would benefit from a clear statement of the company's vision and mission to guide its objectives and future direction.

Slide 5: Technology & IP - Securing the Edge

- Buffer Pitch Deck: Mentions the development of proprietary technology and integrations with major social media platforms.
- "Ace the Pitch" Approach: Highlights technological innovation but could further emphasize any unique intellectual property that protects their platform.

Slide 6: Business Model - Sustaining Value Creation

- Buffer Pitch Deck: Describes a freemium model with a clear path from free to paid plans, detailing conversion rates and user acquisition costs.
- "Ace the Pitch" Approach: Clearly outlines how Buffer generates revenue and maintains sustainability, fitting well with the recommended format.

Slide 7: GTM Motion - Entering the Market

- Buffer Pitch Deck: Discusses initial growth strategies and key metrics of user acquisition and retention.
- "Ace the Pitch" Approach: Provides an overview of market entry but could be enhanced by detailing specific go-to-market strategies and expansion plans.

Slide 8: The Competition - Outlining the Battlefield

- Buffer Pitch Deck: Lists key competitors in the social media management space and differentiates Buffer's offerings.
- "Ace the Pitch" Approach: Effectively outlines the competitive landscape and how Buffer differentiates itself from competitors.

Slide 9: Market Traction - Demonstrating Early Success

- Buffer Pitch Deck: Showcases user growth, revenue metrics, and integration milestones.
- "Ace the Pitch" Approach: Successfully demonstrates market traction, providing concrete data that builds investor confidence.

Slide 10: The Financials - Mapping the Numbers

- Buffer Pitch Deck: Provides financial metrics including revenue run rate and lifetime value (LTV) of customers.
- "Ace the Pitch" Approach: Details financial performance, though could be expanded with more comprehensive financial forecasts.

Slide 11: The Risks - Addressing Potential Hurdles

- Buffer Pitch Deck: Risks are not explicitly discussed.
- "Ace the Pitch" Approach: Would benefit from identifying potential risks and outlining mitigation strategies to provide a more rounded view.

Slide 12: The Contingencies - Planning for Uncertainties

- Buffer Pitch Deck: No specific contingencies are discussed.
- "Ace the Pitch" Approach: Discussing contingency plans for unexpected market or operational challenges would demonstrate strategic foresight.

Slide 13: The Team - The Drivers of Success

- Buffer Pitch Deck: Introduces the founding team and highlights their backgrounds and achievements.
- "Ace the Pitch" Approach: Effectively showcases the team, enhancing investor confidence in their capability to execute the business plan.

Slide 14: Target Milestones - Setting the Roadmap

- Buffer Pitch Deck: Lists past milestones and hints at future goals, including API development and user growth targets.
- "Ace the Pitch" Approach: Would benefit from a more detailed roadmap with specific, time-bound milestones for future development.

Slide 15: The Ask - Securing Strategic Investment

- Buffer Pitch Deck: The specific investment ask and terms are not detailed.
- "Ace the Pitch" Approach: Clearly stating what Buffer is seeking from investors and how it will be used would be crucial for securing funding.

III. Case Study: Airbnb

https://tinyurl.com/airbnb-casestudy

Let's delve into Airbnb's pitch deck. The analysis evaluates how Airbnb's presentation to potential investors aligns with the structured guidelines outlined in "Ace the Pitch," providing a clear framework for effective startup pitching. Airbnb, a company that has revolutionized the way people think about travel accommodations, uses its pitch deck not only to secure financial investment but also to articulate its mission of creating unique, authentic travel experiences through local hosting.

This study aims to uncover the strengths and potential areas for improvement in Airbnb's pitch strategy, assessing its effectiveness in communicating key aspects such as the problem it solves, market validation, and its innovative solution. By dissecting each slide according to "Ace the Pitch" criteria, we gain insights into how well Airbnb managed to convey its value proposition, competitive advantage, and financial potential to secure strategic investment.

Slide 1: The Problem - Unveiling Market Gaps

- Airbnb Pitch Deck: Highlights the disconnect that travelers experience with cities and cultures when staying in traditional hotels and the inconvenience of the current methods of booking local stays.
- "Ace the Pitch" Approach: Effectively identifies a clear gap in the travel market, setting a strong foundation for introducing their innovative solution.

Slide 2: Market Validation - Confirming the Demand

- Airbnb Pitch Deck: Shows market demand through statistics of listings on temporary housing sites and the number of travelers engaged in various global events.
- "Ace the Pitch" Approach: Provides solid evidence of market demand, confirming that there is a significant interest in alternative lodging solutions.

Slide 3: The Solution - Bridging the Gap

- Airbnb Pitch Deck: Describes their platform that connects travelers with hosts offering unique local stays, thereby enhancing the travel experience by integrating into the local culture.
- "Ace the Pitch" Approach: Clearly presents a direct solution to the identified problem, bridging the gap with a user-friendly platform that benefits both hosts and travelers.

Slide 4: The Company - Vision and Mission

- Airbnb Pitch Deck: While not explicitly stated in the provided material, the overarching theme suggests a mission to revolutionize the travel industry by making authentic travel experiences easily accessible to everyone.
- "Ace the Pitch" Approach: Would benefit from explicitly stating the company's vision and mission to better align with the company's strategic goals.

Slide 5: Technology & IP - Securing the Edge

- Airbnb Pitch Deck: The technology aspect is implied through the platform's ability to connect users and process transactions efficiently, but specific details on proprietary technology or IP are not provided.
- "Ace the Pitch" Approach: Could be strengthened by detailing the unique technological innovations and any intellectual property that protects their platform.

Slide 6: Business Model - Sustaining Value Creation

- Airbnb Pitch Deck: Explains their revenue model through service fees charged to hosts and guests.
- "Ace the Pitch" Approach: Clearly outlines how Airbnb generates revenue, demonstrating a sustainable business model that scales with the number of users.

Slide 7: GTM Motion - Entering the Market

- Airbnb Pitch Deck: Not specifically covered in the slides provided.
- "Ace the Pitch" Approach: Should include strategies for market entry, growth, and how they plan to capture and expand their customer base.

Slide 8: The Competition - Outlining the Battlefield

- Airbnb Pitch Deck: Lists competitors and highlights Airbnb's competitive advantages, such as being first to market and offering a unique user experience.
- "Ace the Pitch" Approach: Effectively outlines the competitive landscape and Airbnb's differentiation factors, which is crucial for positioning in a crowded market.

Slide 9: Market Traction - Demonstrating Early Success

- Airbnb Pitch Deck: Provides metrics on listings and user engagement, showing significant traction.
- "Ace the Pitch" Approach: Demonstrates early success effectively, which is critical for building investor confidence.

Slide 10: The Financials - Mapping the Numbers

- Airbnb Pitch Deck: Specific financial data is not provided in the slides.
- "Ace the Pitch" Approach: Would benefit from detailed financials including past revenue figures, projections, and key financial metrics to provide a clearer picture of financial health and growth potential.

Slide 11: The Risks - Addressing Potential Hurdles

- Airbnb Pitch Deck: Not addressed in the slides provided.
- "Ace the Pitch" Approach: Identifying and discussing potential risks and their mitigation strategies would complete this section, offering a more rounded view of the business landscape.

Slide 12: The Contingencies - Planning for Uncertainties

- Airbnb Pitch Deck: No specific contingencies are discussed.
- "Ace the Pitch" Approach: Discussing contingency plans for unexpected market or operational challenges would demonstrate foresight and strategic planning.

Slide 13: The Team - The Drivers of Success

- Airbnb Pitch Deck: Introduces key team members, focusing on their roles and contributions.
- "Ace the Pitch" Approach: Effectively showcases the team, enhancing investor confidence in their ability to execute the business plan.

Slide 14: Target Milestones - Setting the Roadmap

- Airbnb Pitch Deck: Future goals and expansion plans are implied but not explicitly detailed.
- "Ace the Pitch" Approach: Clearly defined, time-bound milestones for future development would provide a clearer roadmap for investors.

Slide 15: The Ask - Securing Strategic Investment

- Airbnb Pitch Deck: The specific investment ask and terms are not detailed.
- "Ace the Pitch" Approach: Clearly stating what Airbnb is seeking from investors, how it will be used, and the expected impact on the company's growth would be crucial for securing funding.

IV. Case Study: Stripe

https://tinyurl.com/stripe-casestudy

In this analysis, let's delve into Stripe's pitch deck presented during their venture capital funding round. Stripe, a company at the forefront of simplifying online payments, has positioned itself as a key innovator in the financial technology sector. This case study methodically examines how Stripe's pitch aligns with the structured guidelines provided in "Ace the Pitch," assessing its effectiveness in conveying the company's strategic vision, market opportunity, and technological advancements.

The pitch deck is an essential tool in Stripe's strategic arsenal, designed to articulate not only the vast potential of their offerings but also to underscore the robustness of their business model and the scalability of their technology.

Slide 1: The Problem - Unveiling Market Gaps

- Stripe Pitch Deck: Identifies inefficiencies in traditional payment systems that are not optimized for the internet age, addressing the complexity and inaccessibility for many businesses, especially developers, to easily integrate payments into their platforms.
- "Ace the Pitch" Approach: Clearly outlines significant market gaps that Stripe intends to address, effectively setting the stage for their solution.

Slide 2: Market Validation - Confirming the Demand

- Stripe Pitch Deck: Implies market validation by highlighting the extensive need across various industries for better payment solutions that support global e-commerce growth.
- "Ace the Pitch" Approach: While direct statistical validation is limited, the broad implication of need across multiple sectors suggests strong market demand.

Slide 3: The Solution - Bridging the Gap

- Stripe Pitch Deck: Presents Stripe as a comprehensive, developer-first payments platform that simplifies the integration of financial services into any internet business.
- "Ace the Pitch" Approach: Clearly describes how Stripe's platform solves the identified problems by making payment processing straightforward, secure, and scalable.

Slide 4: The Company - Vision and Mission

- Stripe Pitch Deck: Articulates a mission to increase the GDP of the internet by removing barriers to online commerce.
- "Ace the Pitch" Approach: The vision and mission are inspirational and ambitious, effectively conveying Stripe's overarching goals.

Slide 5: Technology & IP - Securing the Edge

- Stripe Pitch Deck: Discusses its advanced technological infrastructure and continuous innovation in payment processing technology.
- "Ace the Pitch" Approach: Adequately highlights the proprietary technology and intellectual property that provide Stripe a competitive edge in the market.

Slide 6: Business Model - Sustaining Value Creation

- Stripe Pitch Deck: Describes a scalable business model that benefits from network effects as more businesses use the platform.
- "Ace the Pitch" Approach: Clearly explains how Stripe generates revenue through transaction fees, showcasing a sustainable and scalable business model.

Slide 7: GTM Motion - Entering the Market

- Stripe Pitch Deck: Not explicitly detailed, but the global scale and continuous rollout of new features imply a strategic, phased market entry.
- "Ace the Pitch" Approach: More explicit details on market entry strategies would enhance this section.

Slide 8: The Competition - Outlining the Battlefield

- Stripe Pitch Deck: Does not explicitly detail competition, focusing more on Stripe's unique value proposition.
- "Ace the Pitch" Approach: Would benefit from a direct comparison to key competitors, highlighting Stripe's differentiators.

Slide 9: Market Traction - Demonstrating Early Success

- Stripe Pitch Deck: Indicates traction by noting the platform's widespread adoption across multiple countries and industries.
- "Ace the Pitch" Approach: Successfully demonstrates market acceptance, though more specific metrics or growth rates would provide deeper insights.

Slide 10: The Financials - Mapping the Numbers

- Stripe Pitch Deck: Lacks specific financial figures or projections in the provided slides.
- "Ace the Pitch" Approach: Including detailed financials, projections, and current financial health would strengthen investor confidence.

Slide 11: The Risks - Addressing Potential Hurdles

- Stripe Pitch Deck: Risks are not discussed.
- "Ace the Pitch" Approach: Identifying and addressing potential risks and mitigation strategies is crucial for a well-rounded pitch.

Slide 12: The Contingencies - Planning for Uncertainties

- Stripe Pitch Deck: No contingencies are discussed.
- "Ace the Pitch" Approach: Discussing contingency plans for unexpected market or operational challenges would demonstrate foresight and preparedness.

Slide 13: The Team - The Drivers of Success

- Stripe Pitch Deck: Introduces key team members with their roles and expertise.
- "Ace the Pitch" Approach: Effectively showcases the experienced leadership team capable of executing the company's vision.

Slide 14: Target Milestones - Setting the Roadmap

- Stripe Pitch Deck: Not explicitly covered, though ongoing feature rollouts imply ongoing development goals.
- "Ace the Pitch" Approach: Clear articulation of future milestones would help illustrate the company's strategic direction.

Slide 15: The Ask - Securing Strategic Investment

- Stripe Pitch Deck: The specific investment ask and terms are not detailed.
- "Ace the Pitch" Approach: Clearly stating what Stripe is seeking from investors and how it will be used would be critical for securing funding.

V. Case Study: Uber

https://tinyurl.com/ubercab-casestudy

In the landscape of startup innovation, Uber's early pitch deck from 2008 offers a glimpse into the foundational strategy of a company destined to revolutionize urban mobility. This case study dissects Uber's initial pitch to investors, exploring how the then-emerging startup articulated its vision, addressed market inefficiencies, and proposed a transformative solution that promised to redefine the traditional cab service.

This review not only traces the strategic outline of Uber's early business model but also evaluates the clarity and impact of their presentation against best-practice pitching techniques. Through this examination, the aim is to extract valuable lessons on crafting compelling narratives that resonate with potential backers, providing insights that are relevant not only to entrepreneurs but also to investors seeking to understand the pivotal components of a successful startup pitch.

Slide 1: The Problem - Unveiling Market Gaps

- Uber Pitch Deck: Discusses inefficiencies in the current cab system, including outdated technology and the medallion system, which limits the quality of service and increases costs.
- "Ace the Pitch" Approach: This slide should clearly define the problem being solved. Uber effectively highlights the inefficiencies and customer pain points in the existing cab services, setting a solid foundation for their solution.

Slide 2: Market Validation - Confirming the Demand

- Uber Pitch Deck: The problem slide indirectly suggests market validation by highlighting the inefficiencies and the public's growing dissatisfaction with current cab services.
- "Ace the Pitch" Approach: While Uber indicates a need for change, direct market research or data to back up these claims would strengthen this section.

Slide 3: The Solution - Bridging the Gap

- Uber Pitch Deck: Introduces UberCab as a fast, efficient on-demand car service utilizing modern technology to improve the customer experience and reduce operational inefficiencies.
- "Ace the Pitch" Approach: The solution is well-articulated, addressing the problems mentioned and explaining how Uber's model offers a significant improvement.

Slide 4: The Company - Vision and Mission

- Uber Pitch Deck: This aspect is not explicitly covered in the slides provided.
- "Ace the Pitch" Approach: Ideally, this slide should clearly state the company's vision and mission to guide its objectives and future direction.

Slide 5: Technology & IP - Securing the Edge

- Uber Pitch Deck: Mentions the use of mobile technology, intelligent dispatch, and GPS tracking.
- "Ace the Pitch" Approach: Demonstrates the technological advantage and innovations that Uber brings to the table, but could further highlight any proprietary technology or intellectual property.

Slide 6: Business Model - Sustaining Value Creation

- Uber Pitch Deck: Discusses a membership-based model, digital hailing, and an efficient, tech-driven service system.
- "Ace the Pitch" Approach: Clearly explains how Uber plans to generate revenue and scale operations, fitting well with the recommended format.

Slide 7: GTM Motion - Entering the Market

- Uber Pitch Deck: Details about market entry strategy are limited, but the service launch in specific cities suggests a focused rollout.
- "Ace the Pitch" Approach: More details on the initial market entry strategy and subsequent expansion plans would enhance this slide.

Slide 8: The Competition - Outlining the Battlefield

- Uber Pitch Deck: Implicitly addresses competition by highlighting the shortcomings of existing cab services and differentiating Uber's tech-driven approach.
- "Ace the Pitch" Approach: A direct comparison with major competitors and a clearer outline of Uber's competitive edge would provide more depth.

Slide 9: Market Traction - Demonstrating Early Success

- Uber Pitch Deck: Not specifically covered in the slides provided.
- "Ace the Pitch" Approach: This slide should showcase early achievements, user growth, or pilot results to demonstrate market traction, which is missing.

Slide 10: The Financials - Mapping the Numbers

- Uber Pitch Deck: Financials are not detailed in the initial slides.
- "Ace the Pitch" Approach: Should include key financial metrics, projections, and current financial status to give investors a clear view of the financial health and potential growth.

Slide 11: The Risks - Addressing Potential Hurdles

- Uber Pitch Deck: Risks are not explicitly discussed.
- "Ace the Pitch" Approach: Identifying potential risks and outlining mitigation strategies would complete this section effectively.

Slide 12: The Contingencies - Planning for Uncertainties

- Uber Pitch Deck: No specific contingencies are mentioned.
- "Ace the Pitch" Approach: Discussing contingency plans for unexpected challenges would demonstrate foresight and planning.

Slide 13: The Team - The Drivers of Success

- Uber Pitch Deck: The team's composition and credentials are not detailed.
- "Ace the Pitch" Approach: A slide dedicated to the team, highlighting their backgrounds and roles, would bolster confidence in their capability to execute the business plan.

Slide 14: Target Milestones - Setting the Roadmap

- Uber Pitch Deck: Future goals and expansion plans are briefly touched upon.
- "Ace the Pitch" Approach: Clearly defined, time-bound milestones for future development would provide a clearer roadmap for investors.

Slide 15: The Ask - Securing Strategic Investment

- Uber Pitch Deck: Specific funding needs and terms are not detailed.
- "Ace the Pitch" Approach: Clearly stating the investment sought, the terms, and how it will be used to fuel growth is crucial for securing investment.

VI. Case Study: Alto Pharmacy

https://tinyurl.com/alto-casestudy

In the rapidly evolving landscape of digital health services, Alto Pharmacy's $200 million Series E pitch deck offers a compelling glimpse into how innovative companies are transforming traditional industries through technology. This case study delves into Alto Pharmacy's strategic presentation to investors, showcasing their disruptive approach to the pharmaceutical industry.

With a focus on improving customer experience and operational efficiency, Alto aims to reshape pharmacy services by leveraging advanced technology and customer-centric solutions.

This analysis examines how Alto's pitch deck aligns with the structured guidelines provided in "Ace the Pitch," assessing the effectiveness of their communication regarding market gaps, the innovative solutions provided, and their robust business model. By exploring the nuances of Alto's approach, from the initial problem identification to their growth strategies and financial projections, this case study aims to extract key insights that can aid other startups in crafting compelling narratives for their own funding endeavors.

The goal is to understand how Alto Pharmacy has not only captivated the interest of investors but also set a new standard for service delivery within the pharmacy sector.

Slide 1: The Problem - Unveiling Market Gaps

- Alto Pharmacy Pitch Deck: The deck highlights inefficiencies in the current pharmacy experience, such as inconvenience, lack of pricing transparency, and manual administrative processes.
- "Ace the Pitch" Approach: Alto effectively identifies and communicates the problems faced by patients and providers, setting a strong foundation for their solution.

Slide 2: Market Validation - Confirming the Demand

- Alto Pharmacy Pitch Deck: Demonstrates demand through statistics on medication waste, inefficiencies in traditional pharmacies, and poor customer satisfaction scores for existing services.
- "Ace the Pitch" Approach: Alto uses robust data to validate the market need, aligning well with this guideline by showcasing extensive industry research and customer pain points.

Slide 3: The Solution - Bridging the Gap

- Alto Pharmacy Pitch Deck: Details their next-generation pharmacy platform that offers price transparency, convenient delivery, and improved patient-provider communication.
- "Ace the Pitch" Approach: The solution is clearly outlined and directly addresses the problems described, showcasing how Alto's innovative platform and services bridge the existing market gaps.

Slide 4: The Company - Vision and Mission

- Alto Pharmacy Pitch Deck: This aspect is not explicitly covered in the specific slides reviewed.
- "Ace the Pitch" Approach: Typically, a clear vision and mission statement should be articulated to guide the company's objectives and strategies.

Slide 5: Technology & IP - Securing the Edge

- Alto Pharmacy Pitch Deck: Highlights their proprietary technology platform, designed to manage the end-to-end process of prescription filling and delivery efficiently.
- "Ace the Pitch" Approach: This slide effectively communicates Alto's technological advancements and intellectual property, emphasizing their unique position in the pharmacy sector.

Slide 6: Business Model - Sustaining Value Creation

- Alto Pharmacy Pitch Deck: Explains their business model, which includes capital-efficient geographic expansion and a robust tech infrastructure supporting their operations.
- "Ace the Pitch" Approach: Alto presents a clear and sustainable business model, well-aligned with this guideline by detailing how they generate revenue and manage operational costs.

Slide 7: GTM Motion - Entering the Market

- Alto Pharmacy Pitch Deck: Describes their market entry strategy, which involves expanding into high-value U.S. markets using a hub-and-spoke model to scale efficiently.
- "Ace the Pitch" Approach: This approach to market entry is well-documented, demonstrating a strategic plan for rapid expansion.

Slide 8: The Competition - Outlining the Battlefield

- Alto Pharmacy Pitch Deck: Brief mentions of the competitive landscape are made, comparing traditional and online pharmacies.
- "Ace the Pitch" Approach: While some competitive elements are addressed, a more detailed competitive analysis could further strengthen this section by explicitly comparing features and strategies against key competitors.

Slide 9: Market Traction - Demonstrating Early Success

- Alto Pharmacy Pitch Deck: Highlights their rapid growth, high NPS scores, and significant ARR, indicating strong market acceptance.
- "Ace the Pitch" Approach: Alto effectively demonstrates early market traction by showcasing impressive growth metrics and customer satisfaction levels.

Slide 10: The Financials - Mapping the Numbers

- Alto Pharmacy Pitch Deck: Provides current financial performance and positive trends in contribution margin and ARR.
- "Ace the Pitch" Approach: Detailed financial projections or historical financials would enhance this slide, offering investors clearer insights into financial health and future potential.

Slide 11: The Risks - Addressing Potential Hurdles

- Alto Pharmacy Pitch Deck: Not specifically covered in the slides reviewed.
- "Ace the Pitch" Approach: Discussing potential risks and mitigation strategies is essential for a comprehensive pitch. Including this could provide a more balanced view of the business landscape and Alto's preparedness.

Slide 12: The Contingencies - Planning for Uncertainties

- Alto Pharmacy Pitch Deck: No specific contingencies are discussed.
- "Ace the Pitch" Approach: Detailing contingency plans for potential market changes or operational challenges would be beneficial, showing foresight and strategic planning.

Slide 13: The Team - The Drivers of Success

- Alto Pharmacy Pitch Deck: Mentions the team briefly, focusing on their roles and contributions to Alto's development.
- "Ace the Pitch" Approach: A more detailed introduction of key team members, their backgrounds, and specific contributions could further solidify investor confidence in the team's capability to execute the business plan.

Slide 14: Target Milestones - Setting the Roadmap

- Alto Pharmacy Pitch Deck: Discusses future expansion plans and strategic goals.
- "Ace the Pitch" Approach: Outlining clear, time-bound milestones for future development would help clarify the roadmap and expected progress.

Slide 15: The Ask - Securing Strategic Investment

- Alto Pharmacy Pitch Deck: The specific investment ask and terms are not detailed in the reviewed material.
- "Ace the Pitch" Approach: Clearly stating the funding requirements, how the funds will be used, and the expected impact on the company's growth would be critical to secure strategic investment.

VII. Case Study: Udemy

https://tinyurl.com/udemy-casestudy

Udemy's pitch deck offers an insightful view into how the company positions itself as a leader in the online education space. Founded with the mission to improve lives through learning, Udemy provides a platform that empowers both instructors and students by offering a vast array of courses accessible to anyone with an internet connection.

This case study compares Udemy's pitch deck to the structured guidelines provided in "Ace the Pitch," evaluating how effectively each component aligns with best practices for presenting a compelling narrative.

Slide 1: The Problem - Unveiling Market Gaps

- Udemy Pitch Deck: Highlights the challenges in traditional education systems, such as high costs, limited accessibility, and the rigidity of course offerings.
- "Ace the Pitch" Approach: Clearly defines the market gaps, setting the stage for introducing Udemy's innovative solution.

Slide 2: Market Validation - Confirming the Demand

- Udemy Pitch Deck: References the growing demand for online learning platforms, supported by market trends and increasing internet penetration.
- "Ace the Pitch" Approach: Provides solid data to validate the market demand, aligning well with the guideline to confirm the need for Udemy's services.

Slide 3: The Solution - Bridging the Gap

- Udemy Pitch Deck: Presents Udemy as a platform offering a wide range of accessible, affordable, and self-paced online courses.
- "Ace the Pitch" Approach: Clearly describes how Udemy's solution addresses the identified problems, effectively bridging the market gap.

Slide 4: The Company - Vision and Mission

- Udemy Pitch Deck: States the mission to improve lives through learning, emphasizing commitment to providing accessible education.
- "Ace the Pitch" Approach: Effectively communicates the company's vision and mission, guiding its strategic objectives.

Slide 5: Technology & IP - Securing the Edge

- Udemy Pitch Deck: Mentions proprietary technology for publishing and managing courses but lacks discussion on intellectual property.
- "Ace the Pitch" Approach: Could be strengthened by detailing the unique technological innovations and intellectual property that provide a competitive edge.

Slide 6: Business Model - Sustaining Value Creation

- Udemy Pitch Deck: Explains the revenue model, including aggressive revenue sharing with instructors and pricing control.
- "Ace the Pitch" Approach: Outlines how Udemy generates revenue and sustains its business model, aligning well with best practices.

Slide 7: GTM Motion - Entering the Market

- Udemy Pitch Deck: Discusses plans to expand into new markets like India and the government sector.
- "Ace the Pitch" Approach: Provides an overview of market entry strategies, but more specific tactics would enhance this section.

Slide 8: The Competition - Outlining the Battlefield

- Udemy Pitch Deck: Lists competitors and differentiates Udemy's offerings by its extensive course selection and flexible learning model.
- "Ace the Pitch" Approach: Effectively outlines the competitive landscape and Udemy's differentiators.

Slide 9: Market Traction - Demonstrating Early Success

- Udemy Pitch Deck: Highlights milestones such as user growth and course offerings.
- "Ace the Pitch" Approach: Successfully demonstrates market traction with concrete data, building investor confidence.

Slide 10: The Financials - Mapping the Numbers

- Udemy Pitch Deck: Does not provide detailed financial projections or current financial performance.
- "Ace the Pitch" Approach: Including detailed financials, projections, and key metrics would strengthen this section.

Slide 11: The Risks - Addressing Potential Hurdles

- Udemy Pitch Deck: Mentions some disadvantages but does not comprehensively address risks.
- "Ace the Pitch" Approach: Identifying potential risks and outlining mitigation strategies would provide a more balanced view.

Slide 12: The Contingencies - Planning for Uncertainties

- Udemy Pitch Deck: No specific contingencies are discussed.
- "Ace the Pitch" Approach: Discussing contingency plans for unexpected market or operational challenges would demonstrate strategic foresight.

Slide 13: The Team - The Drivers of Success

- Udemy Pitch Deck: Introduces the founding team, highlighting their backgrounds.
- "Ace the Pitch" Approach: Effectively showcases the team, enhancing investor confidence in their capability to execute the business plan.

Slide 14: Target Milestones - Setting the Roadmap

- Udemy Pitch Deck: Lists some future plans but lacks specific milestones.
- "Ace the Pitch" Approach: Clearly defined, time-bound milestones for future development would provide a clearer roadmap for investors.

Slide 15: The Ask - Securing Strategic Investment

- Udemy Pitch Deck: Does not specify the investment ask or terms.
- "Ace the Pitch" Approach: Clearly stating what Udemy is seeking from investors and how it will be used would be crucial for securing funding.

VIII. Case Study: SendGrid

https://tinyurl.com/sendgrid-casestudy

SendGrid's pitch deck, created for their early funding rounds, showcases the company's mission to simplify email delivery for businesses by solving common problems such as deliverability, scalability, and lack of insight. Founded by Isaac Saldana, Jose Lopez, Tim Jenkins, and Kyle Kermgard, SendGrid aims to provide a reliable, scalable, and easy-to-use email service. This case study compares SendGrid's pitch deck to the structured guidelines provided in "Ace the Pitch," evaluating how effectively each component aligns with best practices for presenting a compelling and investor-ready narrative.

Slide 1: The Problem - Unveiling Market Gaps

- SendGrid Pitch Deck: Highlights key issues with transactional email such as deliverability, scalability, lack of insight, and the time-consuming nature of managing email systems.
- "Ace the Pitch" Approach: Clearly defines significant market gaps, effectively setting the stage for introducing SendGrid's solution.

Slide 2: Market Validation - Confirming the Demand

- SendGrid Pitch Deck: References the high volume of transactional emails sent daily and the substantial impact of non-delivery on businesses.
- "Ace the Pitch" Approach: Provides solid data to validate the market demand, aligning well with the guideline to confirm the need for SendGrid's services.

Slide 3: The Solution - Bridging the Gap

- SendGrid Pitch Deck: Describes their cloud-based email service that offers easy integration, hosted service, and zero coding, solving the issues of deliverability, scalability, and insight.
- "Ace the Pitch" Approach: Clearly describes how SendGrid's solution addresses the problems, effectively bridging the market gap.

Slide 4: The Company - Vision and Mission

- SendGrid Pitch Deck: Implies their mission to make email delivery easy but lacks a clear, explicit statement of vision and mission.
- "Ace the Pitch" Approach: Would benefit from a statement of the company's vision and mission to guide its objectives and direction.

Slide 5: Technology & IP - Securing the Edge

- SendGrid Pitch Deck: Discusses the technology behind their email service, including deliverability solutions and scalability features.
- "Ace the Pitch" Approach: Highlights technological innovation but could be strengthened by detailing intellectual property protections.

Slide 6: Business Model - Sustaining Value Creation

- SendGrid Pitch Deck: Explains the tiered pricing model based on email volume and features, detailing different service levels.
- "Ace the Pitch" Approach: Outlines how SendGrid generates revenue and sustains its business model, aligning well with best practices.

Slide 7: GTM Motion - Entering the Market

- SendGrid Pitch Deck: Discusses customer acquisition strategies including direct ad campaigns, social media marketing, and partnerships with hosting companies.
- "Ace the Pitch" Approach: Provides an overview of go-to-market strategies, but more specifics would enhance this section.

Slide 8: The Competition - Outlining the Battlefield

- SendGrid Pitch Deck: Lists competitors and differentiates SendGrid's offerings by its comprehensive deliverability, scalability, and metrics.
- "Ace the Pitch" Approach: Effectively outlines the competitive landscape and SendGrid's differentiators.

Slide 9: Market Traction - Demonstrating Early Success

- SendGrid Pitch Deck: Highlights progress with 100 paying customers, over 150 million emails sent, and 3 million emails sent per day.
- "Ace the Pitch" Approach: Successfully demonstrates market traction with concrete data, building investor confidence.

Slide 10: The Financials - Mapping the Numbers

- SendGrid Pitch Deck: Provides financial goals such as raising $300k and achieving $60k in monthly recurring revenue with 400 customers.
- "Ace the Pitch" Approach: Includes financial targets but could benefit from more comprehensive financial projections and historical financial performance.

Slide 11: The Risks - Addressing Potential Hurdles

- SendGrid Pitch Deck: Does not explicitly discuss risks.
- "Ace the Pitch" Approach: Identifying potential risks and outlining mitigation strategies would provide a more balanced view.

Slide 12: The Contingencies - Planning for Uncertainties

- SendGrid Pitch Deck: No specific contingencies are discussed.
- "Ace the Pitch" Approach: Discussing contingency plans for unexpected market or operational challenges would demonstrate strategic foresight.

Slide 13: The Team - The Drivers of Success

- SendGrid Pitch Deck: Introduces the founding team, highlighting their backgrounds and relevant experiences.
- "Ace the Pitch" Approach: Effectively showcases the team, enhancing investor confidence in their capability to execute the business plan.

Slide 14: Target Milestones - Setting the Roadmap

- SendGrid Pitch Deck: Lists financial goals and customer acquisition targets but lacks specific, time-bound milestones.
- "Ace the Pitch" Approach: Clearly defined milestones for future development would provide a clearer roadmap for investors.

Slide 15: The Ask - Securing Strategic Investment

- SendGrid Pitch Deck: Specifies the investment needed and how it will be used to grow the business and achieve the set financial goals.
- "Ace the Pitch" Approach: Clearly states the investment ask and intended use, aligning well with best practices.

IX. Case Study: Front

https://tinyurl.com/front-casestudy

Front's $10 million Series A pitch deck provides an insightful look into how the company presents itself as a transformative solution for business communication. By consolidating all external communications into a collaborative inbox, Front aims to enhance productivity and efficiency for teams across various industries. This case study rigorously compares Front's pitch deck to the structured guidelines provided in "Ace the Pitch," assessing its effectiveness in communicating the company's vision, market opportunity, and strategic direction.

Slide 1: The Problem - Unveiling Market Gaps

- Front Pitch Deck: Identifies the inefficiencies and non-collaborative nature of traditional email systems, which are not designed for business use, leading to poor productivity and high error rates.
- "Ace the Pitch" Approach: Clearly defines significant market gaps, effectively setting the stage for introducing Front's solution.

Slide 2: Market Validation - Confirming the Demand

- Front Pitch Deck: References the massive volume of business emails sent daily and the high growth rate of email usage, highlighting the critical need for a more efficient system.
- "Ace the Pitch" Approach: Provides solid data to validate the market demand, aligning well with the guideline to confirm the need for Front's services.

Slide 3: The Solution - Bridging the Gap

- Front Pitch Deck: Describes Front as a collaborative, integrated, and unified email client that centralizes all communications and integrates with third-party applications.
- "Ace the Pitch" Approach: Clearly describes how Front's solution addresses the identified problems, effectively bridging the gap.

Slide 4: The Company - Vision and Mission

- Front Pitch Deck: States their mission to rebuild email for businesses, emphasizing collaboration, integration, and transparency.
- "Ace the Pitch" Approach: Effectively communicates the company's vision and mission, guiding its strategic objectives.

Slide 5: Technology & IP - Securing the Edge

- Front Pitch Deck: Highlights proprietary technology for integration, analytics, and a robust API, but lacks details.
- "Ace the Pitch" Approach: Highlights technological innovation but could be strengthened with details of IP.

Slide 6: Business Model - Sustaining Value Creation

- Front Pitch Deck: Explains the revenue model based on per-seat licensing, with different pricing tiers based on features and usage.
- "Ace the Pitch" Approach: Outlines how Front generates revenue and sustains its business model, aligning well with best practices.

Slide 7: GTM Motion - Entering the Market

- Front Pitch Deck: Discusses acquisition strategies, including organic growth, sales, and marketing, and details their focus on customer word-of-mouth and repeatable strategies.
- "Ace the Pitch" Approach: Provides an overview of go-to-market strategies, but more specifics would enhance this section.

Slide 8: The Competition - Outlining the Battlefield

- Front Pitch Deck: Lists competitors and differentiates Front's offerings by its collaborative features, integrations, and ease of use.
- "Ace the Pitch" Approach: Effectively outlines the competitive landscape and Front's differentiators.

Slide 9: Market Traction - Demonstrating Early Success

- Front Pitch Deck: Highlights significant milestones such as user growth, MRR growth, and low churn rates, demonstrating traction.
- "Ace the Pitch" Approach: Successfully demonstrates market traction with concrete data, building investor confidence.

Slide 10: The Financials - Mapping the Numbers

- Front Pitch Deck: Provides financial projections, revenue growth, and detailed expense breakdowns, thereby showcasing a clear path to profitability.
- "Ace the Pitch" Approach: Includes detailed financials and projections, aligning well with the guidelines recommended to map out financial health.

Slide 11: The Risks - Addressing Potential Hurdles

- Front Pitch Deck: Does not explicitly discuss risks.
- "Ace the Pitch" Approach: Identifying potential risks and outlining mitigation strategies would provide a more balanced view.

Slide 12: The Contingencies - Planning for Uncertainties

- Front Pitch Deck: No specific contingencies are discussed.
- "Ace the Pitch" Approach: Discussing contingency plans for unexpected challenges would demonstrate strategic foresight.

Slide 13: The Team - The Drivers of Success

- Front Pitch Deck: Introduces the founding team and key executives, highlighting their backgrounds and relevant experiences.
- "Ace the Pitch" Approach: Effectively showcases the team, enhancing investor confidence in their capability to execute the business plan.

Slide 14: Target Milestones - Setting the Roadmap

- Front Pitch Deck: Lists product roadmap milestones and future development plans, including new platforms and integrations.
- "Ace the Pitch" Approach: Clearly defined milestones for future development provide a clear roadmap for investors.

Slide 15: The Ask - Securing Strategic Investment

- Front Pitch Deck: Specifies the $10 million investment needed to accelerate growth and outlines how the funds will be used.
- "Ace the Pitch" Approach: Clearly states the investment ask and intended use, aligning well with best practices.

X. Case Study: Coinbase

https://tinyurl.com/coinbase-casestudy

Coinbase's pitch deck, created to secure funding for its early stages, provides a comprehensive look into the company's mission to make digital currency accessible and easy to use for everyone. Founded by Brian Armstrong and Fred Ehrsam, Coinbase aims to offer a secure platform for buying, selling, and managing cryptocurrencies. This case study rigorously compares Coinbase's pitch deck to the structured guidelines provided in "Ace the Pitch," evaluating how effectively each component aligns with best practices for presenting a compelling and investor-ready narrative.

Slide 1: The Problem - Unveiling Market Gaps

- Coinbase Pitch Deck: Identifies the complexity and insecurity associated with buying, storing, and using digital currencies like Bitcoin, which deters mainstream adoption.
- "Ace the Pitch" Approach: Clearly defines significant market gaps, effectively setting the stage for introducing Coinbase's solution.

Slide 2: Market Validation - Confirming the Demand

- Coinbase Pitch Deck: References the growing transaction volume of $2 million USD per day and the rapid adoption of Bitcoin, highlighting the increasing interest in digital currencies.
- "Ace the Pitch" Approach: Provides solid data to validate the market demand, aligning well with the guideline to confirm the need for Coinbase's services.

Slide 3: The Solution - Bridging the Gap

- Coinbase Pitch Deck: Describes Coinbase as a secure app for buying, selling, and storing digital currencies, with an easy-to-use interface and robust security features.
- "Ace the Pitch" Approach: Clearly describes how Coinbase's solution addresses the identified problems, effectively bridging the market gap.

Slide 4: The Company - Vision and Mission

- Coinbase Pitch Deck: Implies a mission to create an open financial system for the world, making digital currency accessible and safe.
- "Ace the Pitch" Approach: Effectively communicates the company's vision and mission, guiding its strategic objectives.

Slide 5: Technology & IP - Securing the Edge

- Coinbase Pitch Deck: Highlights the security and ease-of-use of their platform but does not detail specific intellectual property protections.
- "Ace the Pitch" Approach: Highlights technological innovation but could be strengthened with details of IP protections.

Slide 6: Business Model - Sustaining Value Creation

- Coinbase Pitch Deck: Explains the revenue model through transaction fees and the buying and selling of digital currencies.
- "Ace the Pitch" Approach: Clearly outlines how Coinbase generates revenue and sustains its business model, aligning well with best practices.

Slide 7: GTM Motion - Entering the Market

- Coinbase Pitch Deck: Discusses international expansion and use cases like remittance, e-commerce, and micro-transactions.
- "Ace the Pitch" Approach: Provides an overview of go-to-market strategies, but more specifics would enhance this section.

Slide 8: The Competition - Outlining the Battlefield

- Coinbase Pitch Deck: Lists competitors and differentiates Coinbase's offerings by its user-friendly interface and robust security features.
- "Ace the Pitch" Approach: Effectively outlines the competitive landscape and Coinbase's differentiators.

Slide 9: Market Traction - Demonstrating Early Success

- Coinbase Pitch Deck: Highlights significant milestones such as user growth and transaction volumes, showing a daily growth rate of 20%.
- "Ace the Pitch" Approach: Successfully demonstrates market traction with concrete data, building investor confidence.

Slide 10: The Financials - Mapping the Numbers

- Coinbase Pitch Deck: Provides early financial metrics such as transaction volumes and revenue projections.
- "Ace the Pitch" Approach: Includes financial targets but could benefit from more comprehensive financial projections and historical financial performance.

Slide 11: The Risks - Addressing Potential Hurdles

- Coinbase Pitch Deck: Does not explicitly discuss risks.
- "Ace the Pitch" Approach: Identifying potential risks and outlining mitigation strategies would provide a more balanced view.

Slide 12: The Contingencies - Planning for Uncertainties

- Coinbase Pitch Deck: No specific contingencies are discussed.
- "Ace the Pitch" Approach: Discussing contingency plans for unexpected market or operational challenges would demonstrate strategic foresight.

Slide 13: The Team - The Drivers of Success

- Coinbase Pitch Deck: Introduces the founding team, highlighting their backgrounds and relevant experiences.
- "Ace the Pitch" Approach: Effectively showcases the team, enhancing investor confidence in their capability to execute the business plan.

Slide 14: Target Milestones - Setting the Roadmap

- Coinbase Pitch Deck: Lists future plans and growth targets but lacks specific, time-bound milestones.
- "Ace the Pitch" Approach: Clearly defined milestones for future development would provide a clearer roadmap for investors.

Slide 15: The Ask - Securing Strategic Investment

- Coinbase Pitch Deck: Specifies the investment needed to scale operations and expand the user base.
- "Ace the Pitch" Approach: Clearly states the investment ask and intended use, aligning well with best practices.

APPENDIX A

TAM, SAM, SOM: DEFINITIONS AND HOW TO CALCULATE

Total Available Market (TAM)

TAM refers to the total market demand for a product or service. It represents the entire revenue opportunity available if one achieves 100% market share in the area one plans to operate.

How to Calculate TAM:

Top-Down Approach: This method uses industry reports and market research to identify the total market size. For example, if reports state the global market for smartphones is $250 billion, that would be the TAM for a company entering this space.

Bottom-Up Approach: This method calculates TAM by multiplying the number of potential customers by the average revenue per customer. For example, if there are 10 million potential customers and the expected spending per customer annually is $100, then TAM = 10 million × $100 = $1 billion.

Value-Theory Approach: This method estimates TAM based on how much value the new product or service will add to the market. For example, if a product saves each customer $500 per year and there are 2 million potential customers, the TAM would be 2 million × $500 = $1 billion.

Serviceable Available Market (SAM)

SAM is the portion of the TAM targeted within your geographical reach and is relevant to the technologies, products, or services that your company is offering.

How to Calculate SAM:

Market Segmentation: Define the segment of the TAM that can realistically use your product or service due to geographic, regulatory, or other constraints.

Calculation Example: If you are selling a product that is only compliant with regulations in the European market, and the European market constitutes 30% of the global market, then SAM = 30% of TAM.

Serviceable Obtainable Market (SOM)

SOM is the portion of the SAM that you can capture. It considers current competition and realistic market share based on your business model, capacity, and marketing strategy.

How to Calculate SOM:

Market Share Estimation: Estimate the market share you can realistically achieve in the SAM considering your business strengths, competition, and marketing reach.

Calculation Example: If you believe you can capture 5% of the SAM in the first year, and your SAM is $200 million, then SOM = 5% of $200 million = $10 million.

APPENDIX B

NORTH STAR METRICS OF POPULAR COMPANIES

Slack: Number of Paid Teams - This metric indicates the number of teams that subscribe to Slack's paid plans, highlighting its value in professional settings.

Netflix: Watch Time per User - This metric measures the total time users spend watching content, indicating user engagement and content popularity.

HubSpot: Weekly Active Teams - This metric tracks the number of teams actively using HubSpot's tools on a weekly basis, highlighting its utility in team-based settings.

Instagram: Daily Active Users - This metric indicates the number of users who interact with the platform daily, reflecting user engagement and the platform's daily relevance.

Salesforce: Average Records per Account - This metric measures the average number of records (e.g., customer contacts, sales data) managed per account, showing the depth of use and integration into business processes.

Quora: Total Questions Answered - This metric tracks the number of questions answered on the platform, highlighting the platform's utility in providing valuable information.

Spotify: Total Time Spent Listening - This metric tracks the cumulative time users spend listening to music or podcasts, reflecting user engagement with audio content.

Cameo: Number of Orders - This metric counts the number of personalized video messages ordered, reflecting engagement and popularity.

Shopify: Total Active Merchants - This metric indicates the number of merchants actively using the Shopify platform to sell products, reflecting its success in attracting and retaining business users.

Pinterest: Weekly Active Pinners - This metric measures the number of users who actively create or save pins weekly, showing user involvement and content engagement.

Medium: Total Time Spent Reading - This metric captures the time users spend reading articles, indicating the platform's effectiveness in engaging readers.

Plaid: Total Bank Accounts Linked - This metric counts the number of bank accounts linked to the service, demonstrating its reach and integration with users' financial lives.

Coinbase: Monthly Transacting Users - This metric tracks users who perform transactions each month, indicating active user engagement and platform reliability.

Robinhood: Total Funded Users - This metric measures the number of users who have funded their accounts, reflecting trust and willingness to invest through the platform.

Zoom: Weekly Hosted Meetings - This metric measures the number of meetings hosted on the platform each week, indicating its critical role in remote communication.

Airbnb: Monthly Nights Stayed - This metric tracks the number of nights guests stay per month, indicating the platform's usage and the trust hosts and guests place in Airbnb.

Uber: Weekly Completed Rides - This metric measures the number of rides completed each week, showing the platform's efficacy and reliability.

APPENDIX C

TYPICAL REASONS WHY INVESTORS PASS

It's Too Early

Investors often seek companies that have passed the initial concept stage and have begun generating revenue. The in-revenue stage reduces investment risk and validates the business model.

No Niche Understanding

Companies need to thoroughly understand their target market and customers. A lack of this understanding can deter investors who might see the business as potentially unsuccessful due to misaligned market fit.

Portfolio Overlap

Investors avoid investing in companies that directly compete with other entities in their portfolio to prevent conflicts of interest. Researching an investor's existing portfolio is crucial to avoid such overlaps.

Concerns About Your Team

Investors look at the team behind the company, focusing on areas like expertise, experience, and internal dynamics. Concerns in these areas can be a significant deterrent.

No Business Plan

A clear and thorough business plan is essential. It demonstrates the company's roadmap and shows preparedness. A lack of a business plan suggests a lack of direction and strategy.

Lack of Trust in Your Idea

Founders must prove that their business idea is unique and viable through thorough market research. Investors need to believe in both the idea and the founder's ability to execute it.

No Scalable GTM Channels

Investors look for companies that have identified and tested marketing channels that can scale. This ensures that the invested capital will be used for growth rather than experimentation without direction.

Ignorance of KPIs

Knowing key performance indicators (KPIs) is crucial. A deep understanding of these metrics correlates with better management and success, and it's something investors want to see.

Failing to Understand Competition

A comprehensive competitive analysis is crucial. Founders must understand how competitors are addressing the same problem and how their solution is better or different.

Short Runway

Companies should have enough funds to operate for at least 12 months post-investment. This demonstrates to investors that the business can sustain itself and grow without immediate additional funding.

No Skin in the Game

Investors prefer founders who are fully committed to their business, which often means working full-time and having personal finances invested in the company.

Understanding these points can help you increase the likelihood of securing investment.

FURTHER INSIGHTS AND INSPIRATION

This section offers additional resources to complement the insights shared in "Ace the Pitch." I've drawn inspiration from a variety of sources to enrich the guidance provided throughout this book. The links below are particularly influential pieces that I found invaluable. I encourage you to explore this content further to deepen your understanding of how to ace your pitch!

The Arc Product-Market Fit Framework by Sequoia
https://www.sequoiacap.com/article/pmf-framework/

Venture Capital Due Diligence Questionnaire by Kushim
https://edda.co/assets/the_venture-capital_duediligence_questionnaire.pdf

Extending Your Runway by Sequoia
https://www.sequoiacap.com/article/extending-your-runway/

Y Combinator Investment Memo Template
https://visible.vc/templates/yc-series-a-investment-memo-template/

Pitch the way VCs think: by Khosla Ventures
https://www.khoslaventures.com/wp-content/uploads/Pitch-the-way-VCs-think_2019_FINAL.pdf

LinkedIn Series B Pitch Deck by Reid Hoffman
https://www.reidhoffman.org/linkedin-pitch-to-greylock/

Pitch Decks and Templates on Slideshare
https://www.slideshare.net/search?searchfrom=header&q=pitch+deck

THE FINAL PITCH: TURNING YOUR VISION INTO VENTURE VICTORY

As I bring the journey through "Ace the Pitch" to a close, it's important to reflect on the pivotal moments and key learnings that have unfolded across these pages. This book was crafted not just to guide you through creating an effective pitch, but to transform you into a storyteller who captivates and convinces with confidence and clarity. The art of the pitch is not merely a skill, it is an essential tool in the entrepreneur's toolkit, one that bridges the gap between vision and reality, idea and execution.

Throughout this guide, you've encountered various strategies from understanding investor psychology to mastering the narrative arc of your startup story. Each chapter was designed to build upon the last, creating a comprehensive pathway that leads from the drawing board to the boardroom. You now hold the insights necessary to articulate not only what your product does but why it matters in a crowded marketplace.

The pitch is your opportunity to shine, to stand out, and to show potential investors not just the viability of your business, but its potential to disrupt markets and create value. It's about painting a picture so compelling that others can't help but want to be part of your journey. Remember, every pitch is a unique blend of data and story, analytics and emotion, structured around the core pillars you've learned:

- The Power of Preparation: Understanding your audience, tailoring your message, and anticipating questions will set you apart.
- Clarity and Conciseness: Being able to distill complex ideas into simple, compelling messages is an art that will engage and retain investor interest.
- Passion and Persuasiveness: Your enthusiasm can be infectious, and coupling it with a strong value proposition is irresistible.
- The Ask: Clearly and confidently making your funding request, backed by rational and emotive reasons why an investor should commit.

As you step forward from here, use this book not as a one-time read but as a continuous reference. The nuances of each pitch may differ, but the foundational strategies you've learned will remain constant. Whether you're addressing angel investors, venture capitalists, or potential partners, the core principles of "Ace the Pitch" will empower you to present with authority and vision.

Finally, remember that entrepreneurship is a journey of peaks and valleys. The resilience you develop through each pitch, each meeting, each rejection, and each success will define your path forward. Use the feedback and experiences from every pitch to refine your approach, enhance your business model, and sharpen your delivery. This iterative process is what transforms good entrepreneurs into great ones.

I conclude "Ace the Pitch" with a call to action for you, the entrepreneur, to take bold steps toward making your vision a reality. Armed with the knowledge and techniques from this book, embrace your next challenge with the confidence that you are fully equipped to showcase your business idea in its best light. May your pitches be powerful, your endeavors successful, and your innovations transformative.

Here's to your success in capturing minds and markets as you turn your entrepreneurial dreams into reality.

Go forth and conquer!

Made in the USA
Columbia, SC
05 May 2025